Oil City Library

Oil City, Pa.

Memorial Book
in memory of

Mrs. Hannah Levine

presented by
Mrs. Hazel Gunderman
and Mrs. Edith Davis

THE MATCH, THE BOX
AND THE LABEL

THE MATCH, THE BOX AND THE LABEL

Joan Rendell

DAVID & CHARLES
Newton Abbot   London   North Pomfret (Vt)

British Library Cataloguing in Publication Data

Rendell, Joan
    The match, the box and the label.
    1. Matchbox labels—History
    I. Title
    769.5   NC1889

ISBN 0-7153-8352-3

Typeset by ABM Typographics
and printed in Great Britain
by Butler & Tanner Limited, Frome and London
for David & Charles (Publishers) Limited
Brunel House   Newton Abbot   Devon

Published in the United States of America
by David & Charles Inc
North Pomfret   Vermont 05053   USA

CONTENTS

To the memory of all the collectors of yesteryear who sowed the seeds of our great hobby and who were such an inspiration to me and countless others in the early days

INTRODUCTION

This book is intended to serve as an introduction to the gloriously satisfying and intensely interesting hobby of collecting matchbox labels. It can be a passing phase or a lifetime's study — just as it suits one. However, experience has shown that the majority of those who lightheartedly take it up as a short-term interest often go on to develop their collections into an absorbing long-term pursuit.

My previous books on this subject have dealt with the story of the match industry in all parts of the world and with the manifold subjects depicted on labels over the years. In order to try to present something different I have this time endeavoured to cover a broader spectrum which will give an overall picture of what it is about.

There have been various names coined at various times for collectors of matchbox labels. I use none of them in this volume, the reason being that none of them describes the subject correctly or adequately. The most popular one — phillumenist — is built up from Greek and Latin words and thus is a hybrid word, something which is not altogether desirable at any time, but furthermore it translates as 'lover of light'. Since matchbox labels do not themselves provide light and since the collectors of matchbox labels and associated items do not concentrate on the strength of the flame or any aspect of the power to produce light as such, the word is totally irrelevant to the subject. I envisage a lover of light as one who collects electric light bulbs, candles and so on, for the pure joy of the light they produce!

Therefore in nearly fifty years of collecting — from very early childhood, through to maturity — I have always referred to the hobby as 'collecting matchbox labels' and to anyone amassing a collection as 'a collector of matchbox labels', so this is how both are described in this volume. I only hope I have been able to put over some of my own enthusiasm for the subject.

Joan Rendell

1

HOW IT ALL STARTED

'Whatever should we do without matches?' A natural enough reaction in modern times but matches have been with us only since 1826, whereas the oldest evidence of the use of fire comes from France and Hungary and dates back more than 500,000 years.

The need to strike a light has always existed and the original ways of doing so were simple but unbelievably tedious; later they became involved as well as tedious — until a chemist in the North of England, one John Walker, invented the friction match.

For several hundred-thousand years the main methods of making fire were by percussion between stones and/or friction between two pieces of wood. Even today, if one has sufficient patience and enthusiasm, it can be demonstrated that rapid friction between two sticks of wood will generate sufficient heat to kindle highly flammable material such as perfectly dry moss or tow, the coarse broken part of hemp or flax that remains after it has been cut and mangled.

The Australian aborigines are expert at getting a light from two sticks by rotating one on another between the palms of the hands but those readers who have had Scout or Guide training will probably be more familiar with the sawing method of one piece of wood against another. Whichever way it is done it is a pretty laborious way of making fire. An even harder way used by primitive peoples and still employed in some parts of the world is the striking together of two stones, usually flints, to generate a spark which will ignite some very flammable material. The process is slightly easier if the flint is struck against a lump of iron material such as pyrite but again it is a very hard way of producing a mere spark. Incidentally, pyrite firestones have been found at Upper Paleolithic sites dating back 12,000–30,000 years.

Nearer our time the ancient Egyptians were still using friction between a piece of hard wood and a piece of soft wood to produce a flame. Although that was 5,000 years ago, the Egyptians' culture was so advanced it is surprising that they had not been able to discover some easier way of getting a light. Terrible difficulties must have arisen in wet weather or damp climates, for even in Egypt the sun does not shine all the time.

Then there was always tinder; the dictionary defines tinder as 'any combustible substance used to kindle fire from a spark' and although today we tend to think of tinder as charred rag, in earlier times it was plant down (the soft hairy down on some plants and/or the featherlike substance by which seeds are transported) and that could include the tow and moss used by earliest man. The fungoid growth on oak and beech trees could also be dried and treated to act as a form of tinder.

Most people connect tinder with household tinder boxes and the almost superhuman effort and patience required, especially on cold winter mornings, to strike a flint against a steel in order to create a spark which would ignite the charred rag in the tinder box and so eventually, by thrusting a sulphur-tipped stick into it, produce a flame. Incidentally these sticks, which look like rather rough and clumsy matches, are sometimes mistaken for early matches, which, strictly speaking, they are not.

In the late eighteenth and early nineneenth centuries things began to advance a little and various ingenious but often wholly impracticable or downright dangerous methods of generating a light were introduced.

Some of the devices used sulphuric acid, phosphorus and even gunpowder. In 1824 Henry Berry's Instantaneous Light Box caused quite a sensation when it was put on the market; it was

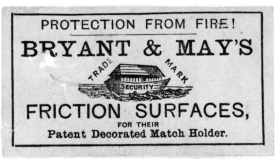

(*top left*) It is many years since paddle steamers were seen on the Mersey; (*top right*) A label from a box of adhesive strips to be stuck onto a metal matchbox holder marketed by Bryant & May in the nineteenth century; (*centre*) Octavius Hunt labels such as this are scarce today; (*bottom*) The cricketer's attire gives an indication of the date of this label. The Victorians also loved a play on words

hailed as a tremendous invention and those able to afford it flocked to buy it. A crudely fashioned match-head coated with a paste made of chlorate of potash, gum and sugar had to be dipped into a small bottle of vitriol and quickly withdrawn, whereupon it would burst into flame. Some of these boxes later had a built-in candlestick, revealed when the side of the box was let down, so that the precious flame could be preserved by lighting the candle. Phosphorus Boxes were slightly less dangerous but still pretty lethal if not used carefully and correctly. In the case of the Phosphorus Box a taper was dipped into a little bottle coated internally with phosphorus and when withdrawn the paper would light if rubbed against a piece of cork or similar material, the friction creating warmth which was sufficient to ignite the phosphorus. The Instantaneous Light Boxes were believed to be a French invention and the first of them appeared in Britain about the year 1810. Henry Berry's type was a marked improvement on the very earliest models in use in Europe. His complicated but ingenious Instantaneous Light Box had elaborate precautions against vitriol being spilt and it took some of the danger out of light boxes.

In 1828 the Promethean Match was patented by Samuel Jones of London, who called his premises in the Strand The Light House. The Promethean Match consisted of a single drop of vitriol in a tiny glass container, wrapped in a piece of paper which was impregnated with a mixture of chlorate of potash, gum arabic and sugar. The whole thing was then rolled into a spill and to obtain a light one nipped the spill with a pair of pliers (not supplied with the matches!) thus snapping the container, releasing the vitriol onto the treated paper and creating a vigorous flame with the most disagreeable smell, the latter fact not being publicised by the manufacturer.

But in the background an unknown chemist called John Walker, living in the town of Stockton-on-Tees in County Durham (now the county of Cleveland), had been quietly labouring away at something that was to revolutionise the industry. He was on the way towards inventing the friction match, the type of thing we use today and cannot imagine not having freely to hand at all times.

Perhaps the strangest thing about John Walker's invention is that he came upon it more or less by chance; one result suggested another

idea to him. Walker had opened his little shop at 59 High Street, Stockton-on-Tees, in 1819 and it was in a room at the back that he conducted his experiments. He seemed to be especially interested in explosive chemicals and kept a meticulous record of his experiments and the results obtained from them.

For years Walker had been working on flame-making techniques. Legend has it that he had been mixing various explosive substances and scraped on the hearth the mixing stick which he had been using. He knew full well that the mixture adhering to the stick had the properties necessary to make it flare, but what gave him the idea for friction matches was that when the substance flared as the stick scraped the hearth, the flame set light to the stick. Instantly John Walker had the vision of sticks being scraped and lighting — in other words what we know today as a match.

This really gave him something on which to work and he applied all his energies to perfecting what he later called his Friction Lights. Walker always kept secret the formula for his match-heads but modern methods of analysis have shown that he used equal parts of potassium chlorate and antimony sulphide made into a paste by the use of gum.

It was in 1826 that John Walker made his great discovery; a year later he was ready to go commercial and he sold the first Friction Lights. The word 'match' he used later. His experimental sticks were made of a kind of cardboard but he soon progressed to wooden splints, cut for him by one of his employees, an old man from the almshouses in Stockton. Walker later employed more old people on this task as the demand for the Friction Lights increased.

The first Friction Lights were sold in cylindrical tins at 1s for 100 plus 2d for the tin, the price including a small piece of glasspaper enclosed in the tin, for use as a friction strip for striking the Lights.

They were slightly alarming in performance. Not all struck satisfactorily but when they did ignite they crackled and sparked and burst into flame quite suddenly. Ladies are reputed to have been warned never to handle them!

Unfortunately John Walker rebutted all attempts to persuade him to patent his invention. Even Michael Faraday, the great chemist and physicist, failed to convince him of the value of taking this step. John Walker always maintained

(left) Hydro-carbon matches and chemical lights came in oval chip boxes to which these labels were affixed; *(right)* A label from the tiny boxes in which these Vestas were sold

that he doubted his invention would be of any real benefit to the public and he could see no need to patent it.

Others, however, were mercenary in their outlook and could see a way of cashing in on someone else's brainchild. In 1829 Samuel Jones launched his Lucifers on the market in a blaze of publicity, the said Lucifers being exact copies of John Walker's Friction Lights.

Jones was a shrewd businessman who had been in the 'light' business for many years; he claimed to have invented the Promethean Match and he could see the potential for such inventions — something which John Walker did not appreciate. So it is little wonder that in Jones's hands the friction match advanced in stature and quality much more quickly than it would have done if only John Walker had been handling it, although it is a matter for regret that such a wonderful invention was purloined almost literally before the very eyes of its inventor. John Walker had a strong objection to the name Lucifers, so in order not to be associated in any way with such matches he ceased selling his own Friction Lights and quite soon after that Lucifers came on to the open market.

However, Jones did not hold the monopoly. For one thing he could not patent his Lucifers since they were, after all, only a copy of someone else's invention and could offer no novel features. This, of course, left the whole thing open to imitation and Jones's near neighbour in the Strand, G. F. Watts, who was also a chemist, soon put on sale an almost identical product which he called Watt's Chlorate Match. He issued printed leaflets declaring his matches to be 'perfectly safe' and 'ignitable by sandpaper only'. The price quoted on the leaflet was 6d per box of 100 matches.

By that time the race was really on and other competitors soon entered the field. A refinement introduced about 1833 was the dipping of the tips of the match splints in sulphur or camphor before they were dipped in the igniting compound, thus making them more combustible.

Inevitably there were various curiosities making an appearance on the market in the early days of the friction match. For instance in 1841 Isaac Davis, an optician, of Poultry in the City of London, invented a friction match attached to a stick of sealing wax and he then went on to produce a similar type of thing which could be used

The wording and pictures on these early British labels give an indication of their date of issue

First there were 'Cigar Lights' (*left c*1880); then when a new technique was introduced for braiding stems they became 'Braided Cigar Lights' and were manufactured up to the late 1920s. Heavy match heads often fell from unbraided or otherwise unsupported stems and could set light to clothes or furnishings

(*opposite*)
(*top left*) The nineteenth-century tiger brand has continued in various modernised versions up to the present day; (*top right*) An early Bryant & May label and (*below*) Congreves were easily ignited and labels for them were often printed in red as a warning; (*centre*) A banderole for a cylindrical box; (*bottom*) An Austrian banderole printed in Greek, French and Arabic

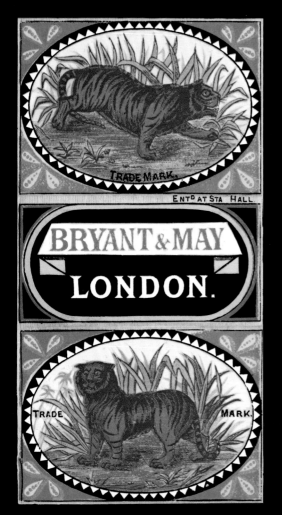

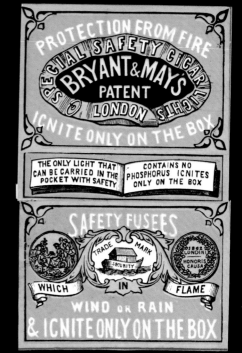

AKTIEBOLAGET GERH-AREHNS
MEKANISKA VERKSTAD
fondée en 1880   Stockholm.

MACHINES POUR LA FABRICATION
DE BOITES D'ALLUMETTES.

BREVETS FR-LUNDGREN·

ALLUMETTES SUÉDOISES
EXPOSITION UNIVERSELLE
PARIS 1900

CONTRIBUTIONS INDIRECTES

GRENADIER 1805

MANUFACTURES DE L'ÉTAT
50 ALLUMETTES-CIRE

SAFETY MATCHES
ATOMIC
REGISTERED   TRADE MARK
HAPBIO TRADING
MANILA
GREAT CHINA MATCH CO LTD HONG KONG

ક પાસ
QUALITY
WIMCO
SAFETY MATCHES

士 勇
中華火柴竹場工廠

TOMMY'S FAVOURITE
SAFETY MATCH
MADE IN AUSTRIA

SWASTIKA
MADE IN   TRADE MARK   SWEDEN
SAFETY MATCHES

UNIVERSAL MATCH CO. FORMOSA·

SAFETY MATCHES
MADE IN SWEDEN

HANUMAN
ORIENTAL
MATCH WORKS. DINDIGUL
SAFETY MATCHES

உதயசூரியன்
PRICE
Re.0-0-6
SRI BRAHADAMBAL MATCH FACTORY
PUDUKKOTTAI

VASUDEV SAFETY MATCHES
MADE   IN   JAPAN
M.MUSABHUY & CO.LTD.,KOBE

JAIGANESH
PRICE
CARMEGAM MATCH WORKS
ELLAIRAMPANNAI

for lighting cigars. He called them Sealing Wax Matches but they were not strictly matches, unless you could call them matches with a dual purpose.

Outside Britain there was also plenty of activity in the realm of match manufacturing once John Walker's invention became known, but progress was not as fast as in England and it was nine years after Walker's discovery before the first acceptable friction match was on sale in the USA. For about a year prior to that home-workers in the USA had been making and selling friction matches of a sort, based on John Walker's Friction Lights.

By 1830 European chemists were making fairly good progress in emulating John Walker and soon after that they were responsible for introducing into match-heads something which was hailed as a boon but proved to be a curse — phosphorus.

The use of phosphorus in match-heads soon revealed dangers and led to the dreaded disease phosphous necrosis of the jaw, popularly known as 'phossy jaw', a terrible complaint among people engaged in making matches and characterised by a rotting of the jaw bone, caused by the action of the phosphorus.

(opposite)
(first row) A rare old Swedish label. At the World Exhibition in Paris in 1900 Gerhard Arehen, a Swedish manufacturer of match-making machines had machines working to demonstrate what they could do. The boxes made by the demonstration machines were given away as souvenirs and this was the label on them; The panoply of war has always held a fascination as depicted on this nineteenth-century French label; The Indian manufacturers warned customers that the quality of their matches was not very good in wartime!
(second row) A 1950s label from Hong Kong remembered Hiroshima; Taiwan is always ready to repulse any attack from mainland China and *(below)* A nineteenth-century patriotic label, Austrian-made
(third row) A modern label from a set depicting semi-religious fairy tales from Formosa (Taiwan); The Wajang mythological and religious puppets of Indonesia; The swastika was a mystic symbol of good luck long before it was adopted as the emblem of the Nazi party in Germany and is shown on a number of labels such as this one from Sweden
(fourth row) An Indian label featuring Hanuman, the Hindu monkey god; Indian labels often portray figures from Hindu mythology; A Japanese label for export to India shows Vasudev, a name of Vishnu; Ganesha, elephant-headed Hindu god on an Indian label

The first phosphoric friction match became available to the public in 1832; it was a joint German–Austrian venture called the Congreve. The name is believed to have been selected in honour of Sir Willian Congreve who died in 1828 and who had invented a famous war rocket; certainly the name was appropriate.

The phosphoric friction match was entirely a European invention and the British market was soon flooded with such matches from Austria and Germany. Congreves were both smaller and more readily ignitable than Lucifers and their imitators but they were also highly inflammable and the slightest friction could cause them to burst into flame, which made them more dangerous. A further 'refinement' was that the side or bottom of the box in which they were sold was either sanded or had a piece of sandpaper stuck on it for the purpose of striking the matches.

Congreves proved remarkably popular in Britain and remained in regular use well into the 1870s before they were finally ousted by the Fusee (intended mainly for the lighting of pipes and cigars) and the Vesta, the latter having a stem made of wax taper. The first patent for such a match was taken out in Britain in 1832 by a patent agent called William Newton. Today we are more accustomed to the wooden-stemmed Vesta but the wax-stemmed kind is still made in quantity in Italy, Spain and some South and Central American countries, and to some extent in Australia and New Zealand.

In 1855 the safety match was developed by J. E. Lundström at Jönköping in Sweden. This was the ultimate in safety as far as combustibility was concerned since the safety match would ignite only when rubbed on a specially prepared striking surface. In the same year the sole British rights for this fine invention were acquired by the famous match firm of Bryant & May.

The safety match is the match as we now know it although strike-anywhere matches are still produced and are, inexplicably, more popular in the north of England than in the south. However, it is estimated that today 90 per cent of matches made throughout the world are safety matches.

It is not the matches themselves that are collected (although some people do like to have examples of as many different types of match as possible) but mainly the labels which adorn the packaging in which the matches are sold. On the other hand, many people prefer really old boxes,

(left) General McMahon, French soldier of Irish descent (1802–73) shown on an old British label *c*1873; *(right)* Sir Walter Scott and 'The Lady of the Lake' on a rare old British label *c*1885

dating perhaps from about 1829 to 1900, kept intact with the original matches. What people collect seems to be mainly related to the amount of storage space in their home that can be allocated to their hobby!

The very first label was presumably used by John Walker for his Friction Lights. One or two of these are supposedly in circulation: one was owned by a famous match firm and another came up for auction when an elderly collector died and his collection put on the market. That little piece of paper fetched £32 some years ago, then a record price for a single matchbox label. But all was not what it seemed. The pieces of paper which it was claimed were used by John Walker to adorn his tins of Friction Lights had printed on them 'As used in the household of His Majesty King William IV'. However, William IV did not come to the throne until 1830 and John Walker stopped selling his Friction Lights before the advent of the Lucifer in 1829. Of course, one could argue that William IV had used Friction Lights before he became king but that was not what was implied on the label and John Walker was not the sort of man to resort to trickery, however innocent, to sell his product.

It is generally accepted that the first genuine matchbox label can be attributed to N. Jones & Co, one of the firms which had produced a slight variation on Walker's invention. In 1830 it started sticking labels on its cardboard boxes of Royal Patent Lucifers. They were pale green, with a crudely printed design of an Englishman and a Scottish Highlander smoking, with the added decoration of two serpents breathing flames; the Royal Arms were patriotically reproduced in the centre of the design. Certainly this was the first-ever pictorial label; if John Walker had a label for his Friction Lights there is no definite proof of what it was actually like or what wording was printed on it.

Strangely, in those far-off days no one seemed to be very anxious to follow the example of N.

Jones & Co. Flowery script and carefully etched lines and swirls were considered more important and for some years N. Jones's bold pictorial label was regarded as somewhat vulgar. The labels on early boxes of Lucifers and Congreves were printed only in black on white paper, the design consisting mainly of geometric lines framing the name of the matches, probably with instructions on how the contents of the box should be used, since matches were still something of a novelty.

By 1880 things had changed. Labels had become so colourful and interesting that people were collecting them and from then on an enthusiam for the hobby grew, slowly at first but rapidly gathering momentum after World War II, until today it is indulged in and enjoyed by thousands of collectors covering an age range from eight to eighty and probably both sides of those figures as well. There is no limit to the number of labels which can be collected and there is also endless scope for specialisation — from pre–1900 British to modern pub signs, from countries like Sweden with an enormous output to countries like Albania with a very limited output. It is pretty certain that whatever type of specialisation is suggested someone somewhere already goes in for it.

Early British labels are one of the most popular groups for specialisation among advanced collectors: forty years ago they were comparatively easy to obtain, now they are becoming harder and harder to locate and the competition for those which do come on the market is keen and determined.

When the British match industry was in its infancy there were hundreds, or probably thousands, of small manufacturers, each with his own brand and presumably his own label, although many of those early brands and labels will never be known now. The same situation applied in the USA and in European countries and in the next chapter we shall see how some of those early matchmakers operated.

2

HOW MATCHES ARE MADE

When one thinks of the sophistication of modern match production with its vast and complicated machinery and its tremendous output, the efforts of the early match manufacturers seem little short of ludicrous. An air of unreality is added by the high-flying names with which some small-time manufacturers dubbed their products, generally made in appalling conditions which would not be considered as even fit housing for cattle these days. Match manufacturers were usually banished to premises remote from other buildings, often on the outskirts of a town, since they were regarded as carrying out dangerous industrial processes; indeed many such premises did burn down sooner or later and numerous tragedies occurred.

There was not much money in match manufacturing in the early days and although a great many people 'jumped on the bandwagon' they did so on a shoestring, with little capital and small chance of being able to rent, buy or build suitable or decent buildings from which to ply their trade. It was therefore not uncommon for work to be carried on in a garret: for instance, William Hiller, who ran a small operation employing young boys in Birmingham for ten years in the 1860s, occupied an upstairs room measuring only 14 sq ft in which the whole matchmaking process was carried out, even down to making the matchboxes. Another Birmingham manufacturer of the same period developed his enterprise in two rooms, one immediately above the other, the connection to the upper one being merely ladder-type stairs, such as in a corn mill or a lighthouse. One can imagine the panic and likely dreadful consequences if fire had broken out in the upper room or if any other such emergency had occurred in the handling of the highly combustible material.

Yet from hovels such as these came matches given such fanciful epithets as Gas Camphor Matches, Hygienic Lights, Double Dip Rock Oil Matches, Chemical Lights, Percussion Lights or the modern-sounding Solar Matches, which might even be a good brand name today. What they lacked in capital and know-how those early manufacturers made up for in imagination!

The highly dangerous process of matchmaking in those days involved the mixing of the deadly phosphorus compound in large earthenware jars, buckets or whatever type of container was available, and stirring the mixture with a thick stick, with no thought of its lethal combustibility and the constant danger to life and limb. Women and children were usually engaged in making boxes for the matches and filling boxes with the finished product; old people were often employed to cut splints. Sometimes in the later nineteenth century the larger manufacturers put splintmaking out to contract, so that there were some people who ran businesses engaged in making match splints only.

The making and labelling of boxes was also an important home industry for the poor, with whole families slaving from dawn to dusk for a wage of a few coppers a week and later having to deliver the fruits of their labour to their employer — for no overtime payment. Of course, all this was not happening in Britain alone. Although it was not until 1835 that an acceptable version of the friction match appeared in the USA some of the early efforts in that country, as well as in Europe, were made under just such deplorable conditions as existed in England.

Prior to 1835 there had been a great deal of experimentation in the USA in an effort to find a chemical method of producing fire and, in fact, scientists and chemists working there on that field may even have been ahead of Europe in some

Three rare and valuable old boxes of British matches which would have been on sale in the mid 1800s

respects. The *Saturday Evening Chronicle* of Cincinnati, dated 14 July 1827, recorded that in 1790 Dr Antoine François Saugrain, a Frenchman who left France at the time of the French Revolution, was making phosphorus lights and obtaining a light by breaking a phosphorus-containing tube, and although such experiments were also being conducted in Britain at that same period, the American version was regarded as being rather more advanced in technique and reliable in use.

In 1830 a French scientist, Dr Charles Sauria, substituted a phosphorus compound for some of the chemicals used in John Walker's Friction Lights. It was on his unpatented discovery that most of the early American match manufacturers are believed to have based their products, as Sauria claimed that his match-heads were more reliable than John Walker's British variety.

As to the manufacture of matches in the USA, in the years 1834 and 1835 many home-workers began making and selling friction matches of a sort and most of such products were not only dangerous to the makers but to the users as well. They were made under the most unscientific conditions as a mainly trial-and-error operation with the most indiscriminate use of chemicals in combinations which were quite likely to blow up in the maker's face or to ignite without warning in the hands of the users. As in Britain there was a dreadful toll of 'phossy jaw' victims amongst the early matchworkers.

William A. Clark of Connecticut was one of the most enterprising of the early American matchmakers and he experimented with the delightful-sounding 'locos focos', which were very thin. flexible splints which would ignite only when they were drawn sharply through a piece of folded sandpaper. They were highly unreliable and when someone did succeed in getting one to light it went off with a quite alarming explosion and emitted a shower of dangerous sparks. Clark used women and children to make boxes by hand in their homes but much later on in his career he invented matchmaking machinery and his son-in-law became one of the founders of the now-great Diamond Match Company of America.

The new invention was held up to some ridicule in certain quarters as the word 'loco' is an American colloquialism for crazy. In fact the name was derived from 'locus' meaning 'place' and 'focus' meaning 'hearth' or 'fire', hence 'light on the spot' or 'light anywhere'. John Walker's name of Friction Lights was far more dignified and probably a much more accurate description!

By the 1860s larger match factories were being opened, matchmaking was becoming big business and gradually the small-time, back-street manufacturers were being squeezed out of the market. With the bigger firms came better conditions for the workers and a British government report published in 1862 said of the Bryant & May factory at

Matchbox labels come in many shapes and sizes. *(top left)* A label from a packet of ten boxes from Iran; *(top right)* A nineteenth-century Austrian label for a pill-box type matchbox; *(bottom left)* A label for a miniature box from Sweden; *(bottom right)* An early Czechoslovakian label from strikers for kitchen matches which fitted into a holder

Bow in east London that it was 'remarkable in the excellence of most of its arrangements both for the health and comfort of the work people', a far cry indeed from the garrets and shed workshops of the 'little' men.

The job itself, however, continued to be laborious and dangerous. Fifteen to twenty different operations were employed in the matchmaking process and most of it was still done by hand. Boxes were still made by outworkers living in the neighbourhood of the factories, usually whole families being engaged in this work: it was certainly not lucrative but it was a living of sorts.

At that time Bryant & May employed about 1,300 workers at the Bow factory, making the matches entirely by hand, and it took a period of forty years for machinery to gradually supplant the manual process in the making of matches and finally of the boxes.

It was in the late nineteenth century that the invention of the continuous matchmaking machine revolutionised the industry. It was adopted at once by the larger manufacturers and enabled them to cut not only the size of their work forces but also to reduce drastically the price of matches on the market. The first continuous matchmaking machine in Britain was installed in 1896 in the Diamond Match Company's factory in Liverpool which five years later was taken over by Bryant & May. The firm installed a similar machine in its main factory at Bow in 1904.

The machine was a remarkable invention for it took blocks of pine wood, cut them into matchsticks and placed the sticks into holes on a steel conveyor belt. This in turn carried the sticks through hot paraffin wax and then through the chemical composition to form the ignitable heads. That was not the end of it either, for the machine also dried the heads and dropped them into the boxes.

Today poplar and aspen are most favoured woods for match-sticks and they are cut mechanically before being fed into match machines. In Britain matchwood is often imported from Canada and Sweden although Bryant & May also has its own forests producing timber for matchsticks. Countries such as Sweden, Russia and so on are of course self-sufficient in timber. In 1975 Bryant & May opened a new splint factory in Australia with capacity for producing some

24,000 million splints a year; the firm also has 800 acres of plantations in Australia.

Matchboxes are now largely made of cardboard instead of the old familiar wooden 'chip' boxes. The cardboard outer covers of matchboxes are called skillets and machines can make 4,000 skillets in an hour.

In 1964 a West German match firm started up in business and it went into the market making plastic matchboxes. These were mainly for advertising purposes at first, being produced for German companies, but in 1966 the firm expanded and began to take on foreign customers; it also produced some souvenir sets with pictures of views of cities, animals, flowers, etc. The innovation was hailed at the time as a breakthrough in matchbox production. In West Germany there were optimistic predictions that the plastic matchbox would take over the world market, that there would be no more wood or cardboard boxes, no more matchbox labels as such and that the future for collectors would hold only plastic boxes. It all sounded very promising but label collectors were, naturally, not over-enthusiastic. Several countries tried out plastic boxes, although it was perhaps significant that none of the world's great match firms went over to them. Predictions proved too optimistic and the plastic matchbox never really took off. Perhaps one reason is that in a litter- and pollution-conscious world people are not anxious to add to the amount of indestructible litter which accumulates in both urban and rural areas. A wooden or cardboard matchbox thrown in the gutter or into a hedge soon disintegrates; a plastic matchbox, like the plastic sacks which now litter the countryside, does not rot and its remains could be kicked about for a very long time. Today plastic matchboxes are usually confined to souvenir packs on sale in tourist areas and are certainly not in general use.

Over the years there has, of course, been a constant seeking after improvements and innovations. There have been new ideas to catch the public's imagination and to widen the market of various firms. One such idea was the StopLite (a match which goes out of its own accord) from the Diamond Match Division of the Diamond International Corporation. It was launched by the American firm in 1976 and is a bookmatch coated below the tip with a fire-resistant chemical: it burns for twelve to fifteen seconds before going

A crude, card envelope-type box for Italian paraffin matches

out. It was hailed as a safety-match-plus in that it would help to cut down the number of fires started by still-burning matches thrown in ashtrays, rubbish bins etc and it would also eliminate the hazard of burnt fingers. It was a splendid idea and no doubt the match has contributed quite significantly to a reduction of fires caused by careless smokers and others using matches.

Incidentally, one of the selling points of the StopLite is that it will counter the old superstition that it was unlucky for three cigarettes to be lighted from one match. This tale arose in the Boer War because a prolonged flame gave the enemy time to take aim and fire and it persisted even more strongly through two world wars and beyond. A StopLite match will not burn long enough for more than one cigarette to be lighted from it (two if you are lucky!) and therefore more can be sold. There are two sides to everything — even matches!

In 1928 Dr Ferdinand Ringer, an Austrian scientist, invented what he called a Firestick, a pencil of compressed chemicals which it was claimed was 'everlasting', providing up to 1,000 strikes before being played out. It was produced commercially but in 1932 production ceased because Ivar Kreuger, the Swedish match 'king' bought the patents and suppressed the Firestick. That idea was detrimental to the sale of ordinary matches!

In 1955 the Czechoslovakian press proclaimed 'Everlasting Fire!'. It was referring to two new match 'inventions' in that country: one was a match which could not be blown out and the other a type of match which smouldered instead of burning and, it was claimed, could generate tremendous heat. The latter got hot enough to start a fire although the match itself never actually flamed and it was purported to be so heat-retaining that if put into a glass of water it would cause the water to boil over. Both matches were packed separately in special paper but they were apparently not a commercial success, since no more was heard of them and they do not seem to have got recognition outside the press of their own country of manufacture.

A short-lived product of the 1920s was self-striking matches. These were sold in flat packs rather like bookmatches in appearance and were manufactured by the Safety Auto-Light Co Ltd of 35 Craven Street, London WC. They were titled Self Striker and were, so it was claimed on the pack, 'Patented in all Principal Countries'. The pack was a strip of folded cardboard stapled on each side to form a pouch and it contained wooden safety matches inserted heads downwards. Printed at the top of the pouch was a line of asterisks and the instructions beneath them said 'Press thumb lightly on Stars and pull'. The match would then rub against abrasive material

Sulphur matches always had red labels and indeed still do in countries where they are still made

inside the pouch and would, it was hoped, emerge lit. This invention was obviously subsidised by advertising and the pack in my own collection publicised Nestlé's Milk. On the front of the pack is a drawing of a boy with his hair standing on end, sitting up in bed (candle, complete with snuffer, on a table by his bedside) and the caption 'Who said Nestlé's Milk?' On the reverse side an advertising panel announces 'Makes Dainty Dishes, Corn Flour Blancmange, Baked and Boiled Custards . . . Etc, Etc. And can be used for all purposes of Fresh Milk'.

These matches appear to have been another nine-days wonder in the match world and certainly never made a great impact on the market. It is strange how so many of these imaginative inventions fell by the wayside in an age when scope for free enterprise was given full rein and the public was always thirsting for something new.

New technology brought other inventions in its wake and the advent of the motor car did not go unnoticed by match manufacturers. Bryant & May was soon on the scene with its Motor Matches — invaluable items for the motorist travelling after dark, for in the early days there was no jumping into the car and switching on the lights. Lamps had to be laboriously lit by hand before setting off, and on cold, wet and windy nights this must have been a nightmare. The Motor Match sold in flat, slide-tray boxes of no-nonsense yellow card with plain black lettering.

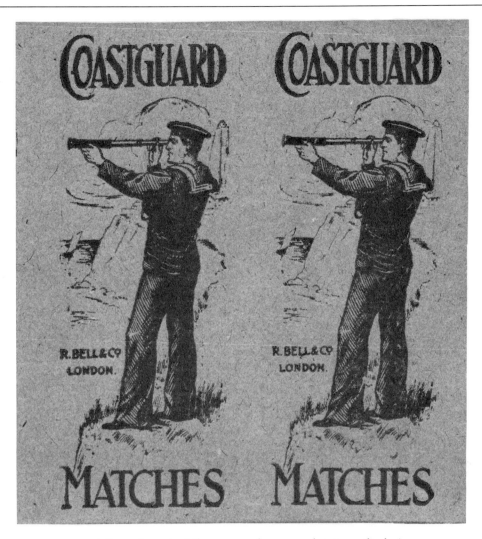

A far cry from the fully automated coastguard stations of today!

The matches, approximately 3½in long and with 1¼in-deep head on stout wooden stems, looked for all the world like sparklers. The caption on the box was reassuring: 'Will flame for 20 Seconds and Keep Alight in the Strongest Wind'. They were sold for 'Motor Car, Cycle and Launch Lamps'.

The search continues for better selling points and economic ways of improving matches. In 1981 Wilkinson Match, of which Bryant & May is a part, patented a new idea for making matches. Wood is now an expensive commodity but it has always been considered the most satisfactory material for match splints because a splint has to be rigid and at the same time sufficiently porous to absorb and retain the wax substance which fuels the flame of the composition top. Bookmatches do, of course, use card for the stems but a bookmatch stem can be infuriatingly 'bendy' and lacks a lot of the qualities and often necessary attributes of the rigid match splint. So Wilkinson Match came up with a splint made of chopped newsprint or cotton waste, mixed with a resin binder and extruded. After that the splint is coated with a layer of material such as cotton, cereal, sawdust or talc. The porous coating is then soaked in paraffin wax before the splints are dipped in the igniting composition. The core is

Bengal matches are coloured pyrotechnic matches but not all such matches were made in Bengal. Ordinary matches were made there too (*left*) and Bengal matches were most commonly made in Germany (*right*)

non-porous but strong and rigid and the porous surface layer provides the necessary boost to ensure a flame.

The concept of the match has lent itself to uses other than making a light and the last word in this chapter must be with two novel variations on the match theme, both of which put in an appearance in the late 1970s. Strike Out was a brand produced in America which could fool anyone into thinking they were going to strike an ordinary light when they withdrew a fusee-type 'match' from its container. Only careful scrutiny of the box revealed that the 'matches' when lighted would act as a deodoriser killing off unpleasant smells and keeping rooms fresh!

At about the same time one could buy in Spain boxes of matches which when struck would give off a repellant designed to discourage and even kill mosquitoes.

3
MATCHBOX LABELS IN WARTIME

The role of the matchbox label in wartime is far more important than may be imagined. Labels have been extensively used for propaganda purposes and wartime conditions have produced some curious specimens, often, of necessity, make-do efforts the like of which will never be seen again.

What may be termed wartime labels can be divided into several types. There is the straightforward propaganda type: popular stock designs have slogans added to them, advocating anything appropriate to the time, from 'Matches are precious, make them last' to a warning that 'Careless talk costs lives'. Special propaganda labels also are often issued and although they seem a puny way of whipping up enthusiasm for the war effort or hate against the enemy, their influence is surprisingly strong and efficacious. Then there is the special-issue type: these may be, for instance, issues for distribution in large military establishments or for specific purposes, such as the boxes of waterproof matches issued to the American soldiers who took part in the D-Day landings in World War II. And there are the labels issued to honour and commemorate leading figures and events of the war years.

Added to all these are many labels which do not strictly fall into any classification but which in one way or another reflect the conditions prevailing during the period in which they are issued. The latter usually become the most desirable from the collecting angle. They are issued in time of stress to meet special circumstances and because of adverse conditions not many are likely to survive. They are usually produced in small quantities and their circulation is of short duration.

It is strange but true that a simple thing like a matchbox emanating from a particular country at a particular time can often tell the enemy far more than it is desirable that he should know about the situation prevailing in the country of origin.

A case in point concerns some labels 'smuggled' out of Bulgaria during World War II. It was understood that Bulgaria was probably suffering privations but no one knew just exactly what things were like, since that country was more or less sealed off from the western world at the time. Then a label collector received some Bulgarian matchboxes and they told a tale which was afterwards confirmed. Bulgaria was so short of essentials that even the supply of printing ink had ceased and the matchboxes were covered with all-round labels of very-poor-quality paper in a variety of colours and entirely free from any printed matter. Other labels in the tiny consignment which reached Britain helped to tell the full story: there were the well-printed, colourful designs which were circulating in Bulgaria when war broke out; these were then superseded by plainer designs printed in one colour only and bearing the state insignia, and wording. A little later these were followed by labels of poor-quality paper with nothing printed on them but the state insignia — put on by a rubber handstamp — and finally the labels were just plain paper, oddments of whatever could be scraped together for the purpose.

Another example of a country with 'make-do' matchboxes which are now rare collectors' items is Eritrea. After the Italian invasion in 1936 the country, never a rich one, was left even poorer and short of the raw materials for everyday living. Matchboxes were therefore made by hand from, ironically, old Italian picture postcards. A small hand-press was used to print a simple outline design of an organ-pipe cactus onto straight strips of poor-quality paper. The strips were then stuck over to seal the postcard boxes A more home-made effort could never be imagined but it served its purpose for a short time. In order to make the boxes a little more attractive the design was printed in black ink on some strips and in red ink on others.

South Africa during World War II ran short of the usual yellow paper on which its matchbox labels were printed, so the Lion Match Co, South Africa's largest match manufacturer, reverted to blue paper. In 1942 the firm issued special war-time labels inscribed 'Don't Talk About Ships' and these were issued in both English and Afrikaans. They were the first to be printed on blue paper and that particular variety is now very scarce. As the shortage of paper continued the well-known Lion brand was also printed on blue paper.

Another South African war measure caused by the shortage of essential materials was the Union Match Co's refill packs of about ninety matches. These were wrapped in brown paper on which was rubber-stamped in red 'Match Refill Union Industries (Pty) Ltd, Germiston', the idea being for the public to conserve boxes and make the striking surface last considerably longer than for just the amount of matches contained in one box. As the striking abrasive for safety matches begins to lose its effectiveness after about fifty matches have been struck on it, it is little wonder that tempers frequently became frayed and South Africans did not regard the refill packets as the brightest idea in the history of match making. Incidently, the National Match Co Ltd ceased production of matches in 1969 and switched to other industries.

The Boer War, too, had an effect on the South African match industry. The now-defunct Star Match Factory at Albertsville opened in 1898 but the outbreak of war in 1899 stopped operations for a time. Another start was made in 1900 but material soon ran out and the factory was obliged to close until the cessation of hostilities in 1902. A South African label of the period was entitled Commando, which has a modern ring about it and was a line drawing of a Boer War battle scene.

During World War II New Zealand match manufacturers were forbidden to use more than two colours in their label designs so that the popular and long-standing Royal Wax Vestas label of the New Zealand Wax Vesta Co Ltd, which was always printed in red, yellow and dark green on white paper, had to have the yellow omitted, after having been printed in three colours since it was first introduced just prior to the 1925–6 Dunedin Exhibition.

It was not only printing which suffered in the match industry because of wartime conditions. In 1944 the Germans, then occupying Belgium, issued an order forbidding Belgian manufacturers from using the red dye which had always charac-terised Belgian match-sticks, together with the yellow heads. So Belgian matches appeared then as white splints with brown heads. It was only a little thing but it made the Belgians very aggrieved at the time.

France was in an even worse position during World War II. In 1942 the collaborating French government announced that matchboxes would be sold only to persons who returned used boxes when making a new purchase; and in Britain the match shortage was so serious in 1941 that a Match Controller (Sir Sydney Chapman) was appointed. He recruited a number of liaison officers whose duty it was to teach the public to save matches, their slogan being 'Make one match do the work of two'. The match manufac-turers did, of course, co-operate to the full and so were born the now-famous and also now-scarce British wartime labels with slogans designed to make the public conscious of the need to conserve matches.

World War II also brought about the intro-duction of what was later developed as a popular commercial line in the USA and elsewhere. For the Normandy landings on D-Day everything was planned down to the last detail and US troops were issued with large boxes of waterproof matches as part of their equipment. The boxes were plain khaki-coloured card on which typical army jargon was printed in black, giving speci-fication and instructions for use of the contents of the boxes. This included the information that the matches would still function after being in water for up to four hours. At that time the compound used in heads of what were then heralded as 'miracle matches' was kept a closely guarded military secret, but soon after the end of the war US match firms started experimenting along the same lines and waterproof matches are now marketed in boxes with bright labels or skillet covers. They meet a great demand from campers, yachtsmen and the like.

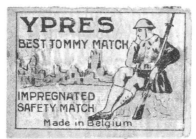

Matchbox labels from World War I: (*first row, left to right*) Russia celebrated the end of the war with this label issued *c*1918; A Dutch label issued after the war featured the Palace of Peace in the Hague; A.N.A. matches were hawked from door to door or sold in the streets by ex-servicemen unable to find work
(*second row*) A Belgian label; In World War I many items of heavy artillery were given names as depicted in this Belgian label
(*third row*) Nurse Cavell was the only heroine to be the subject of a matchbox label; Two more examples of labels from matches sold, often door to door, by ex-servicemen

In World War II there were officially forged matchbox labels. British agents were equipped with everything which they could possibly need on their missions and one of the items which they carried behind the enemy lines was a box of matches. However, the matches were no giveaway. 'Authentic' French and German matches were made by the famous British firm of Bryant & May and in order that they should be perfect copies in every respect special paper, inks, wood and even specially prepared sulphur heads, went into their manufacture. Like everything connected with espionage they were costly — it was estimated that each box cost £5 to produce. So realistic were the labels that today even advanced collectors cannot tell, without written proof,

whether the labels of the 'copied' brands which they have in their collections are the real thing or the now almost priceless spy forgeries. Ironically, it is the one situation in the collecting of labels where forgeries are actually worth money and in most cases worth far more (if authenticated) than the originals from which they were copied.

The Germans do not appear to have been so meticulous in equipping their espionage staff. A Nazi spy landed by submarine in Canada was detected when he dropped a Belgian matchbox on the floor. The unusual box aroused the suspicions of an alert Canadian security man and the spy's arrest and imprisonment soon followed.

Unlikely as it may seem, the dropping of matchboxes from the air can have a profound effect on the fortunes of war. Hitler was first in this field when in the early part of 1938, prior to his March invasion of Austria, he ordered that country to be showered with thousands of matchboxes bearing labels printed in red, black and white and boldly inscribed 'Ein Volk, Ein Reich, Ein Führer' (One People, One Country, One Leader). This slogan was actually filched from a commemorative medal struck on the instructions of the Kaiser in World War I but with the word 'Gott' (God) instead of 'Führer'.

The Americans followed the same course of action in World War II when, after the unsuccessful attempt to regain the Philippines, US planes dropped matchboxes over the islands, each box bearing full-colour reproductions of the American and Philippines' flags and General Douglas MacArthur's promise 'I shall return', with a facsimile of the general's signature beneath it. MacArthur later kept his promise.

Among the most dramatic of all the World War II labels were those issued for the use of members of the Danish underground resistance movement. They bore pictures of a burning swastika and a portrait of Stalin and the wording was an anti-Nazi slogan and hopes for a Russian victory over the Germans. Members of the resistance used them freely but very bravely, for if found with such a box of matches in their possession it was the end of the road for them. The labels were printed in black on mauve paper and at first glance resembled a well-known Danish label of long standing. At one time doubts were expressed by collectors as to whether these were genuine matchbox labels and whether they had actually served the purpose for which they were reputed to have been printed. It was later established, however, that they were genuine and *had* been used by members of the resistance.

'We're all lit up, let Battle commence' was the only wording on a matchbox label issued in India in World War II and intended for distribution to the troops. Apart from the slogan there was a line drawing of an obviously tipsy British soldier wearing full battle dress and lighting a cigarette. Some of the boxes were dispensed to troops in the Far East but the army authorities were apparently not at all happy with the design and wording and the labels were withdrawn. This action brought forth criticism in a letter to a national newspaper in which the writer suggested that the army 'top brass' surely had more important things to do

than censoring matchbox labels. It did, however, immediately catapult this nondescript label into the desirable class and specimens have now become collectors' pieces. Later there was evidence that the army may not have lost financially to any great extent because some of the offending labels turned up on boxes of matches advertising a well-known brand of tea and intended for sale in India — an advertising label had been stuck over the inebriated soldier!

The French, too, had matches specially made for distribution to their troops in World War II. A large consignment of boxes from Lebanon had dark-blue all-round labels with printing in black and carried the words 'Destiné aux troupes. Exempt de banderole'. These were for the use of French colonial troops in North Africa and the quality of the matches was said to be deplorable. The labels were certainly rather crudely printed, cut with a saw-tooth edge and stuck on the outer covers of the boxes with obvious haste and abandon.

The most popular role of the matchbox in wartime is to be printed with slogans, and in World War II this method of disseminating information, warnings and advice was widely used in many countries. We have already discussed examples from Britain, South Africa and the USA. Labels also carried wartime messages to those who were unable to read a slogan, because even the most illiterate person can understand a picture and what could be more graphic than a picture of a bomb with the Japanese flag as a tail fin, falling on a map of the USA? Or an oriental soldier charging with fixed bayonet an unseen enemy, with a big red splash in the background? The message is unmistakable. These more bloodthirsty types of picture were confined to the Far East; the western countries were a little more restrained in their propaganda designs.

British Intelligence, however, did take revenge against the Japanese for the latter's horrific propaganda labels by setting up a jungle printing press overprinting locally manufactured boxes with anti-Japanese messages. A half-million were distributed before the Japanese finally discovered the trick.

Japan suffered from spy mania during World War II and in common with other countries utilised the omnipresence of matchbox labels as a means of alerting the population to the dangers. The best known of that country's 'don't help the

Matchbox labels from World War II: *(first row, left to right)* A controversial label on boxes issued to the troops in India. It was considered by army authorities to be so unsuitable that it was withdrawn and the stock was bought by Brooke Bond which stuck its own label over the top; After the Red Cross was adopted by the Geneva Convention as the symbol of mercy it was not allowed to be used on labels *(centre)* An exception was labels appealing for funds for the Red Cross organisation

(second row) An Indian label warned that the matches were of 'war quality'

(third row) A South African label; Oriental troops were left in no doubt as to what was expected of them by this label from Singapore

(fourth row) A label from Mauritius; Italy glorifies its army in wartime

enemy' labels was one with a picture of a Japanese soldier with a gag over his mouth, but because of wartime conditions when it was issued very few specimens of this label ended up in collections. Incidentally, the Japanese, ever expert at unorthodox business methods (they even gave the name 'Sweden' to a town in Japan some years ago, so that they could sell matches with labels inscribed 'Made in Sweden'!) were said during World War II to sell their mass-produced boxes of matches in occupied China, each label bearing the slogan 'Boycott Japanese Goods' printed across it.

Pictures conveyed suitable messages in some European countries too. Germany produced a label with a shadowy picture of a typical furtive cloak-and-dagger figure and simply the word 'Pssst!', whilst in Finland boxes were distributed with labels which showed merely a pair of lips sealed with a large padlock, another very effective way of putting over the idea.

Between 1914 and 1917 loss of lives was uppermost in everyone's mind but it is doubtful if this was the motive which led to an innovation by Bryant & May and which operated during that period. A free life-insurance policy from £100 to £500 was inserted, like a ticket, in every box of Swan Vestas matches. Among the conditions of this unique insurance were that a box of Swan Vestas must be on the person at the time of the accident and that the death must be due to an injury received whilst travelling. This excluded claims from war-wounded but it is unknown how many, if any, claims were ever made and successfully settled. It was an odd promotion to introduce in wartime but presumably the manufacturers considered it appropriate.

It was in wartime too, in 1916 to be exact, that one of the most famous brandnames ever to appear on a matchbox label came into being. In that year Bryant & May changed the title of its Patent Special Safety Match to the simple Brymay, which it has remained ever since.

The year 1916 did, incidentally, play a significant part in the world of matches for another reason because on 4 April the then Chancellor of the Exchequer, Reginald McKenna, announced in his budget that duty would be put on matches to help pay for the war. The tax has, of course, steadily increased over the years and has never been withdrawn.

Match label brands often used the pathos of

war to appeal to consumers and during the years 1914–18 a brand which sold well was Ypres Best Tommy Match which showed a British soldier gazing reflectively over the ruins of the Belgian town of Ypres, scene of such fierce fighting.

What is it about wartime that inspires new ideas to spring up so abundantly? In the middle of World War II a patent was applied for in respect of a multi-headed match. This provided for an annular or ring-shaped head at regular intervals down one splint. A deep cut was made around each head so that the used part could be broken off, leaving more heads still to be struck from the same splint. This was evidently a genuine attempt to save wood for splints in a time of great shortage but the economics governing the production of such matches prevented them ever going into commercial use and no labels were ever printed for them.

During the same war Holland overcame the shortage of wood for matchboxes by producing cardboard boxes at the National Match Factory at Weert. In 1943 — in a deliberate attempt to spite the occupying Germans, who had imposed strict controls on the match industry as on all other essential industries — the factory issued a set of thirty-six most attractive skillets depicting early methods of transport, ancient Dutch castles, veteran cars and other such escapist subjects which had no connection with war or wartime conditions. The Dutch people regarded these boxes as a triumph, not only over adversity but as a means of showing contempt for an occupying power and the boxes were highly prized. They were finally withdrawn in 1946 but many remain in Dutch homes today as a memorial to the way in which their country rose above occupation by the enemy. The skillets are now also much valued by collectors and well they may be, for the difficulties in obtaining a complete set of all the designs were enormous even at the time when the boxes were on sale in Holland.

In World War II India produced its now well-known Jai Hind (Free India) labels with portraits of Subhas Bose Netaji, a man who raised an army

(opposite)
(top) Patent Vesuvians of c1870; (bottom) Three boxes designed to hold bougies des poches ('pocket candles'), very popular in nineteenth-century Europe. They could be used to light a cigar or pipe, seal a letter or even act as a candle!

to fight in support of the Japanese against the Allies and who later became known as the Indian traitor. During that war India issued a selection of the most extraordinary labels. Some had a crudely drawn picture of a bomb and such strange titles as Bomb Dangerous and Bomb Live and there was even a label entitled The Leader, which many thought bore an unmistakable likeness of Adolf Hitler. Only a small number of the latter labels were circulated and it is believed that this was the only label in the world every to portray Hitler.

Hero worship is common in wartime and, needless to say, great contemporary figures often become popular subjects at the height of their fame and glory. During the Boer War a series of twelve Swedish labels entitled The Union Match was issued which portrayed famous military personalities of the day, including Field Marshal Lord Roberts, Major General Baden-Powell, Major General Lord Kitchener, General Sir Redvers Buller and so on. All the labels in the set are now extremely rare and it is unlikely that many collections can boast a complete set.

The Russo-Japanese war of 1904-5, over the occupation of Korea, brought forth a spate of labels, mainly from Japan but also including a set from Sweden (now much sought-after by collectors) portraying naval and military leaders of both sides.

General Gordon was the subject of a popular brand's label put on sale at the time when he was at the height of his fame. A Swedish issue, it was printed in several variations of paper colour and the design included a picture of a prize medal awarded to the brand at the Calcutta International Exhibition of 1883–4.

(opposite)
(top left) German sulphur matches of *c*1860; *(top right)* A Vesta matchbox of 1848–50, made by Alex Stocker, one of the smaller British match manufacturers; *(bottom)* The author demonstrating the use of a tinder box. The flint is struck against the steel and the resultant spark ignites the tinder in the box; sulphur-tipped sticks are placed in the tinder and, after smouldering, catch alight. A process which requires considerate patience!

Conditions of war always bring great figures to prominence: they may have been unknown before but their outstanding qualities of leadership and courage come to the fore in wartime and they rise from obscurity to become a part of history, so it is not surprising that such persons often become subjects for the ubiquitous matchbox label. Just such a personage was Nurse Edith Cavell who became assured of her niche in history when she was shot by a German firing squad in Brussels in October 1915. One of the heroines of World War I, it has often been said that had she been only imprisoned her name would soon have been forgotten but instead she became an unwitting martyr. Miss Cavell was matron of Belgium's first training school for nurses at the time when the war started and with the invasion of Belgium and the battles of Mons and Charleroi many of the wounded arrived in her training school which had been turned into a hospital. It was then that her remarkable story started as she adopted a Scarlet Pimpernel type of role, assisting British soldiers to escape by 'underground' means across the border into Holland and to freedom. As soon as she was arrested and shot by the Germans she became a national heroine and the first Miss Cavell labels appeared. The matches were made in Belgium and the label centrepiece is a head-and-shoulders drawing of Miss Cavell wearing her nurse's uniform. The labels were used for both paraffin and safety matches and there are several variations of colour in paper and printing — blue and red on white paper, blue and red on yellow paper, and so on. These labels are now much cherished by collectors and are certain to fetch several pounds each when sold in auction. Predictably, because heroism is an emotive subject, especially in retrospect, there were a few protests after the Miss Cavell label was issued, one correspondent to a national newspaper deeming it to be 'in very poor taste'.

During World War II people did not feature much as subjects of label designs. Instead, other subjects applicable to the times were produced by several countries. For instance, a British set of Rank Markings of the Navy, Army and Air Force was a best seller for J. John Masters & Co and collectors worked very hard to complete the set in their albums; today it is a most desirable holding for any collection. In the USA matchbox labels were printed for all the largest military camps and air-force bases, available only to the personnel

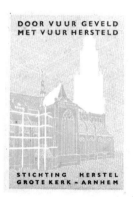

serving in those camps. Several of the labels carried warnings about the consequences of careless talk as well as bearing unit or camp insignia.

British wartime labels from S. J. Moreland's Gloucester factory did valuable service in conveying vital information to the man in the street. The reverse panels of England's Glory and Moreland's Safety Matches vaunted the necessity for and the advantages of National Savings, urged people to dig their gardens for victory, warned against careless talk and boosted the morale of the people with patriotic slogans. However, none was quite so outspoken as a slogan which was printed on the labels for Australian Crown Matches and which said bluntly: 'Don't give Hitler a rest, keep at him all the time'. In 1943 the Nile Match Co of Egypt secured a contract to supply matches to the British troops in Egypt and the design chosen for the label was Sir Winston Churchill's famous V-for-Victory sign.

The aftermath of war often has a telling effect on matches and matchbox labels just as it does on almost everything. After World War I the British press gave prominence to a rather amusing story about the consequences of the French government's announcement that it had taken over a number of wooden huts, formerly used by the American forces, and, with a view to turning the wood into match-sticks, had allocated them to the national match factory. The government regarded this as a very smart move on its part and a quite brilliant way of solving the problem of acute match shortage. The state factory was put to work flat out and produced several million matches but complaints began to filter through about the quality of the matches. It was not until then that it was discovered that the timber of which the huts had been made had been fireproofed by the Americans before the huts were built and it was therefore little wonder that the

After the Italian campaign in Eritrea in 1936 rough matchboxes were made from old Italian picture postcards

wood was not proving ideal for matches!

Another sequel of war was illustrated in a pair of labels (consisting of one subject printed and coloured in two different ways) which followed the break-up of the Austro-Hungarian Empire. The picture on them is of a soldier standing with arm upraised above a drum and other military paraphernalia, flanked by a flag with the double-headed-eagle emblem of Imperial Austria, the national flag of Hungary and the wording 'Remember our comrades in need and their widows and orphans. The profit from these matches is exclusively for the Royal Military Veterans League.' Several other European countries issued labels to raise funds for war victims and their dependants. Another Austro-Hungarian label,

Matchbox labels of World War II: (*first row*) After the war, War Savings became National Savings and received publicity in Britain on Moreland labels; Bryant & May struck a patriotic note on this label for Pilot matches
(*second row*) The Russian occupation of Finland; A label commemorating the partisan fighters in Yugoslavia;
(*third row*) The aftermath of war. A label sold to raise funds towards the rebuilding of Arnhem Cathedral; Two Polish labels depicting instruments of war
(*fourth row*) British Label; Indian label

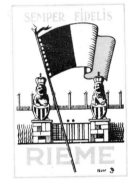

issued about 1897–8, shows a soldier holding aloft a branch of foliage and standing beside a picture of the Emperor Franz Josef. That one was sold 'For the benefit of the relief funds of the Artillery League in North Bohemia'. During World War I itself a set of three charity labels issued in Austria was sold by 'The War Relief Bureau to help relatives of called-up men and people in distress'. The price of the matches included a surcharge which was devoted to the fund.

In Austria, as late as 1947, two years after the end of World War II, boxes of matches were still being sold with plain-paper all-round labels which had long been obsolete. In the same year the Rumanian government seized the Swedish Match Company's £1 million plant in Rumania on the grounds that the factory was making inferior matches to sabotage the post-war 'New Order'; it was announced that matchmaking was to become a state monopoly.

Other countries were also having their difficulties. Can you imagine a box of matches being a highly desirable and valuable gift? It has been so. In August 1947 10,000 boxes of matches were sent to Britain from the Finnish Paper Mills Association as a present to 100 British customers. But the gift never got farther than London's Surrey Docks, where, on the orders of the Customs, the matches became a massive bonfire. Although World War II had ended there were still acute shortages of many commodities in Britain and the Matches Control of the Board of Trade refused an import licence for the gift matches on the basis that the job of the Control Board was to secure even distribution of matches throughout the country and that it would receive a lot of complaints if some people were getting extra boxes. Incidentally, it was not until 2 August 1949 that licences for manufacturers and importers to supply matches were abolished in Britain.

Titles for brands were often derived from wartime subjects and matchbox labels were also used in some cases to help publicise and raise funds for the relief or commemoration of wartime tragedies or events. Representative of these was a set of labels issued in 1957 for the purpose of assisting a fund started in Belgium to make shrines of pil-

The all-round-the-box labels showing rank markings of HM Forces were one of the most popular of all British sets when they appeared in World War II

grimage on the sites of the villages of Rieme and Oostaker in East Flanders. During World War II the Germans established concentration camps for political prisoners in the area and many atrocities took place there. The labels, which were issued in several sets of four, showed pictures of the reconstructed sites — the execution posts, the war memorial, the sites as they looked when the German pulled out and so on.

The collecting of matchbox labels in wartime was far from being brought to a standstill. It did in fact, especially in World War II, mean the acquisition of some very interesting and desirable items for the observant collector. With supplies from Europe cut off, strange foreign brands appeared on the British market from Thailand, India, China, USA etc and included war prizes in

Some of the many labels issued to commemorate German atrocities in Belgium during World War II

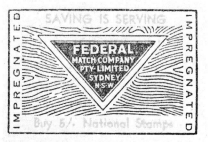

Three Australian labels from World War II

captured stock from Italy. Transient labels, here today, gone tomorrow, to the collector of today they are great treasures, not easily located or obtained. To save paper, stocks of outdated labels were used in Britain, being pasted face downwards on the boxes and several obsolete and comparatively rare old labels turned up in that way. Human nature being what it is, it was not only the collectors who soaked the outer covers of matchboxes to see what the label was underneath. Now one has to search hard and long to find someone who still possesses a wartime 'reversed label' box with its full complement of matches.

'Ill is the wind that profits nobody' is a very old proverb and in the context of the match or 'light' business it is interesting to find how wartime conditions, whilst disastrous to some sections of the match industry were nevertheless the cause of a

boom in others. For instance, the Boer War brought great prosperity to the flint knappers of Brandon in Suffolk because there was an unprecedented demand for what were called 'strike-a-lights' — flints — as the humid climate in certain parts of South Africa made the use of matches uncertain.

That is only one of the strange repercussions which war conditions have had on the match industry. During World War II an American importer was faced with holding a large stock of Two Hammer Brand matches plainly proclaiming on the label 'Made in Japan'. The chances of selling those in a country at war with Japan seemed pretty remote, but the desperate importer employed someone to remove the name of the country of origin from every box before disposing of his stock and cutting his losses!

4

MATCHBOX LABELS
IN RELIGION

These days a link between matchbox labels and religion is rare but it was not so in the past. Over the years labels with a religious aspect have not been a popular subject for specialisation, yet they present a fascinating study. One can recall few leading collectors who sought only labels with a religious connotation. Most of them have now passed on and their collections have been dispersed. A prominent Spanish collector of some forty or so years ago had one of the finest assemblages of religious labels ever put together; when he died it was rumoured that the whole collection, regarded by his relatives to be rubbish, was thrown on a bonfire.

Thankfully, nowadays collectors are more careful and better informed and instructions for the dispersal of collections are often left in wills. However, it is sadly the growing commercialism of the hobby which has engendered this attitude rather than the desire for preservation of something irreplaceable for future generations to enjoy. A growing awareness of the material aspect of label collecting spawns a desire to see what a matchbox label is worth in the market place, more than its desirability as a rare addition to a collection for its aesthetic appeal, and when anything becomes an investment or a commercial undertaking instead of a hobby for pleasure, a lot of the fun goes out of it.

Possibly the most famous of all religious labels belong to a set of sixty familiarly known as the 'Peruvian religious'. For years a great deal of rumour and conjecture has surrounded this handsome set of skillets bearing beautifully reproduced etchings of figures sanctified in the Roman Catholic and other churches — the Mother Mary, Jesus Christ, the Mother and Infant Jesus and many well known and less well known saints. It has been established that these glossy master-pieces were produced in Spain at the end of the nineteenth century and as far as is known no used skillets or made-up boxes exist. The story is that the skillets were printed in Spain and exported to Peru in flat bundles to have abrasive strips added and to be assembled. But when they arrived at their destination the subject of the designs offended the powers-that-be in a strictly Roman Catholic country and the boxes were never assembled; in fact the bundles were never even untied and were supposedly all returned to Spain in the same condition in which they were shipped from Europe. Certainly mint sets of these skillets were contained in many old Spanish collections and have found their way into other collections from time to time. In 1933 press coverage was given in Spain and elsewhere to a find of a large quantity of these skillets in a loft of an old building in Northern Spain believed to have at one time been the headquarters of a printing company. Some of the sets then discovered found their way eventually into collections in Britain and other parts of the world. They were offered among collectors for between £2 10s and £3 10s for a complete set of sixty skillets. Nowadays there are collectors prepared to pay up to ten times that amount for just one set! However, many advanced collectors believe that the story about the find in the loft was complete fabrication, used in the newspapers' so-called 'silly season' when news is scarce. It will probably never be known where the skillets actually came from; suffice it to say that collectors will give their eye teeth to get them!

Among the matchbox labels which over the years have caused collectors the most problems in identification, those from India, China and other Asian countries must be rated high on the list. India has produced a wealth of religious labels but

it must be remembered that in Asian religions there is often a very thin dividing line between religion and mythology. Gods are worshipped as religious figureheads, but they are also mythological figureheads.

Dozens of matchbox labels have been issued picturing Hindu deities. Hinduism is a very complex religion embracing earth worship, sun worship, sky worship, nature worship, mother and father worship, respect for the dead, the mystic association of plants and animals and so on. Thus it can be seen that there is a vast field of subjects for matchbox labels likely to appeal to the Hindu user of matches. So, many labels which perhaps appear meaningless to the Christian have great significance in the Indian market.

Some of the half-human creatures of Hindu mythology descended from being gods themselves to become the companions and vehicles of other gods. One deity will be mounted on a peacock, another on a swan, one will be carried by a bull, another by a goat. The popular Gayatri — Morning, Noon, Evening — set issued by India's largest match firm, WIMCO, some years ago illustrates this theme.

Ganesha, the elephant-headed god, is to the Hindu the god of the universe. He has been pictured on many labels, under his own name, as he is regarded as the god of success and worldly wisdom. He is gentle, calm and friendly, and

Indian matchbox labels: (*first row*) A label depicting Kali, worshipped by millions as the Mother; Hanuman, the Hindu monkey god; A Japanese label for export to India shows Shiva, the great god; Ganesha, elephant-headed Hindu god, shown on a Japanese label for export to India
(*second row*) An old Austrian label for matches to be exported to India; The cow is a sacred animal in India. This label was issued in the 1930s; A label depicting a character in Indian mythology
(*third row*) Hanuman was often depicted on Indian labels; Krishna, a deity of Hinduism, worshipped as the incarnation of Vishnu; Numerology is also important in India
(*fourth row*) A Swedish label for export to India illustrates the story of Ganga, the birth of the river Ganges; An early nineteenth-century label for export to India showing Durvasa, a portion of Shiva the great Hindu god and Sakantula, hermit maiden and daughter of a great holy man in Hindu mythology; Two labels depicting characters in Indian mythology

matches with his picture adorning the box are sure to sell well. Thus match manufacturers play him up to the full.

Probably the best known of the Hindu gods shown on labels is Hanuman, the monkey-god, who has also given his name to the title of match brands. It is said that the religion of Vishnu, the Preserver, will never be able to dispense with Hanuman, who is the Hindu ideal of the perfect servant, the subordinate whose glory is in his own inferiority. He too is very much of a best seller in the match business in India.

The god Maricha was an evil force in Hindu mythology and appeared to Sita, Daughter of the Earth, in the guise of a golden deer. The deer appears on a number of Indian labels and Sita, too, has featured on her own labels on many occasions. Another popular subject is Garuda, the divine bird who haunted the imaginations of all early peoples.

There are so many Indian labels which depict these mythological/religious figures and tales that it would not be possible to list them all in one chapter.

Similarly, Chinese and Japanese labels feature many quasi-religious figures who remain popular despite modern sophistication and progress in their countries of origin.

The preoccupation of the Chinese with mythology, ancestor worship and the festivals connected with these subjects is well known, but pre-1939 Chinese matchbox labels can raise a lot of queries and problems for collectors not familiar with Chinese religion and culture. The bat and deer are both symbols of longevity much beloved by the Chinese and so it is not surprising that they appear on a great many labels, along with other figures from what may seem to occidental eyes the twilight world of semi-religion semi-mythology which characterises oriental thinking. Shou Lao, the god of longevity, is unmistakable on labels issued prior to World War II and subsequent unheavals in China. He is always portrayed as a venerable old gentleman, often holding a Chinese peach, another important symbol of luck and longevity.

Then there are the Eight Immortals; they were pictured on a vast number of matchbox labels issued from about the turn of the century until approximately the outbreak of World War I. These were often brought back to Britain in collections of labels purchased by seafaring men as souvenirs of the Far East, such collections, mounted in albums, being on sale in most Chinese and Japanese ports at the time.

The Eight Immortals form a collection of Chinese deities, representing masculinity, femininity, wealth, poverty, youth, age, aristocracy and plebeianism and denoting the Taoist principles that condemn the worship of power and material things. Like the Hindu gods they can usually be recognised when depicted on labels by their individual characteristics, despite artistic licence in their interpretation. Chung-Li-Ch'uan, a female figure, is nearly always shown carrying a fan; Ho Hsien-Ku is another female figure, mostly shown with flowers, especially a lotus bloom or a ladle; Lu Tung-pin is a rather splendid fellow, wearing a pleated cap and carrying a sword; Li Ti'eh-kua was a most popular label subject, he is ugly in appearance and leans heavily on a crutch; Chang Kuo-hao has a far more benevolent appearance, he is bearded and carries a drum; Ts'ao Kuo-chiu is another bearded character, carrying tickets or placards; Lan Ts'ai-ho, pleasant and rather more attractive, carries flowers, either as a bouquet or in a basket; finally, Han Hsiang-tzu looks slightly forlorn and carries a broken branch.

Japan has a somewhat similar set of characters — its Seven Gods of Good Fortune — and they were portrayed on scores of Japanese labels produced for home consumption from the late nineteenth century to the outbreak of World War I. Like the Chinese issues they invariably carry no identification; usually the only wording on the label is the match manufacturer's name printed in very small letters in order not to detract from the picture. In fact these deities have migrated from China to Japan, where their figurines are more treasured as ornaments in the home than the familiar Three Monkeys (Hear, See, Speak no Evil) at Nikko. The Seven Gods of Good Fortune are the beggar god, Hotei, the most popular and most often depicted on labels, always happy and fond of children; Ebisu, the lucky fisherman, pure of heart and content with a simple life; Jurojiu, the god of longevity, a venerable old man and another popular label subject; Benton, unmistakable with her lyre, the goddess of beauty and art; Daikoku, god of good fortune for farmers; Fukuroku, god of deep learning, always shown with staff and scroll; and Bishamon the warrior god, symbolising courage. Other members of the

Japanese pantheon featured frequently on matchbox labels in the past: now they have lost much of their appeal and possibly some of their glory and they are not such remarkable best sellers as they used to be; in fact they seldom appear at all on modern Japanese labels, if they do appear it is usually on special souvenir labels printed to attract tourists.

The Indian firm of WIMCO had a factory in Burma and was sympathetic to its customers' beliefs and interests. A favourite subject was the mythical beast called Chinthe, a strange creature, somewhat dog-like in appearance but with a misshapen head and forbidding expression, part god, part legend. This figure also appeared on labels printed in Japan for export to Burma.

Figures from Greek and Roman mythology have featured as the subjects for matchbox labels from many different countries. In their time these shadowy figures were worshipped as gods and goddesses. They too can be very confusing to identify. For instance, Juno, sister and consort of Jupiter, who has given her name to match brands (and, of course, labels) from Austria and Finland among others, can be portrayed in several guises. As Juno Regina she is depicted standing with sceptre, patera (a flat dish for pouring out libations), veil and peacock; as Juno Sospita she is armed with a spear and shield; as Juno Lucina she carries a child in her arms and has two children at her feet. She is also sometimes shown with a child in her arms and a flower in her hand, which symbolises the circumstances in which she conceived Mars. Artemis, twin sister of Greek god Apollo, has appeared on several Austrian labels in the past and also on a classical-looking modern Greek label which ten years ago was about the only brand available in Greece. She was a highly skilled huntress and is usually portrayed with bow and arrows, accompanied by a hind or a dog.

(first row) The Wajang mythological and religious puppets of Indonesia; The Japanese god Hotei; Ebisu, the happy fisherman, one of the Japanese gods of Good Fortune
(second row) Li Ti'eh-kua, one of the Chinese Eight Immortals; Hotei, the Japanese beggar god
(third row) Two labels depicting Fukuroku, the Japanese god of Deep Learning
(fourth row) Bishamon, the Japanese warrior god; Shou Lao, god of Longevity; Japanese portrayal of Jesus and Mary *(bottom)* Another of the once-popular Japanese symbolic labels

One of the famous set of skillets known as the 'Peruvian Religious' set

Atlas was another of the mythical Greek gods who meant so much to a pagan people. He was punished by Zeus for taking part in the revolt of the Titans and was condemned to stand forever before the Hesperides on the edge of the world, carrying upon his shoulders the vault of the heavens. He is notably the subject of an Austrian label from the early 1900s which portrays him faithfully. Helios (the Sun) was the subject of another Austrian label about the same time and he has also featured on labels from other countries. He was said to have been drowned in the ocean by his uncles, the Titans, and then elevated to the sky where he became the luminous sun spreading radiance over all.

India was the master of the so-called religious slogan, which to the western way of thinking seems such a curious thing to put on a matchbox label. A brightly coloured pseudo-replica of the old Wills Gold Flake cigarette packets for Fear God matches was regarded as quite blasphemous in the 1930s, especially as it exhorted the customer to 'Always use "Fear God" Superior Quality Damp Proof Safety Matches'. And a military drum horse in all its finery, carrying an energetically drumming military man (complete with bearskin) hardly seemed an appropriate illustration for 'Remember God Damp Proof Safety Matches'. Another Indian custom which somewhat offended westerners earlier this century was the association of religion with the Indian superstitions and beliefs regarding numerology. 'No Religion Greater than Truth' was a popular slogan which appeared on 999 and 888 labels for matches produced in India.

Uproar in the Commons and outraged correspondence to *The Times* were examples of the furore caused by a simple matchbox label in the 1930s when some Jesus Christ labels were imported into Britain from Japan. The label design

was of Jesus Christ, portrayed with noticeably oriental features, apparently walking or floating on clouds. It was quite tastefully coloured in yellow on grey but it was bound to cause trouble in a Christian country. To add insult to injury it even had a spelling mistake — 'Manufactured by Shyosei Co Osaka Japan'. Questions were asked in Parliament and as a result it was banned from sale and stocks called in. To be fair, no blame can be attached to the Japanese manufacturers: undoubtedly they thought that Christ would be a popular subject in a Christian country and presumably even the importer had no idea of the turmoil it would cause.

India also ran into trouble some years ago with a label entitled 'Buddha', showing a picture of the venerable figure and with the inscription 'Made for Burma'. Although it was intended for Burma the first consignment of this issue from the Sivakasi Kaliswari Colour Match Works at Sivakasi in Southern India landed in what was then Ceylon (now Sri Lanka) and immediately caused a row. It was banned from sale almost immediately and rumour had it that some heads rolled for allowing it into the country at all. In 1948 a similar situation occurred in Israel because

St Antony on a Portuguese label

a label printed and issued there showed a mosque and Islamic symbols. It highly offended the Moslem population and was banned because it offended religious sensibilities. All these labels are today much sought after collectors' items and repose only in the longer standing collections, where they are highly prized.

Strangely, what could have been one of the most controversial of all religious labels appears to have passed unnoticed; certainly there is no record of it ever having caused any comment. It is a rare, twentieth-century, highly glazed label from Italy. There is no wording on it but it is a reproduction of a seventeenth-century Italian engraving of the Resurrection showing Christ emerging from the sepulchre and facing Pontius Pilate's Roman soldiers who were guarding the tomb. Perhaps because it was a reproduction of an important artistic work it was considered allowable, despite being used for a throwaway item.

Another aspect of religion in connection with matchbox labels is the manufacture of matches on a commercial scale by a religious organisation, mainly as an act of charity and concern for an underprivileged section of society but also as a means of propagating its beliefs. A now much sought after example is the Lights in Darkest England brand manufactured and marketed at the end of the nineteenth century by the Salvation Army.

At that time the dreadful 'phossy jaw' was relentlessly attacking people — mostly women —

engaged in the making of matches. Its victims invariably died after the most appalling suffering. In order to combat this terrible scourge among the sweated labour force, particularly in the East End of London, the Salvation Army set up a match factory of its own to manufacture matches under better and safer conditions than those prevailing at the time. It was a bold and imaginative project although it was not a financial success (it did, in fact, lose money despite all the moral support given to it from The British Match Consumers' League).

After 1918, when Czechoslovakia emerged as a newly formed country, Bishop Josef J. Strossmeyer, a leading church figure in the days of the Austro-Hungarian Empire, launched a crusade for funds for Czechoslovakian Catholic Schools and several labels were printed and put on boxes of matches sold to further this cause. In 1948 Belgium issued labels for boxes of matches sold to aid a fund for sending Catholic missionaries to Africa and elsewhere. In 1975 the Salvation Army stuck specially printed labels around boxes of matches in an appeal for funds towards the cost of rebuilding the Salvation Army Citadel in Great Yarmouth, Norfolk, to create a community centre. Fourteen thousand such labels were printed at the Army's own printing works and a national supermarket chain presented two cartons of Russian matches on which the labels could be stuck. They were sold between 1975 and 1977 and presumably achieved their target.

5

LABELS IN ADVERTISING

One cannot say that the matchbox label was seen immediately as an effective advertising medium but once the potential was recognised it was, and still is, exploited to the full.

The early match manufacturers had no thoughts but to perfect and market their products. John Walker, for instance, did not use a label at all for his first sales and at that time the only use of a label was to give instructions on the new ways of getting a light, something of which many people were extremely cautious.

The first advertising came in the form of printed leaflets, usually distributed by hand, which promoted and explained the matches, as G. F. Watts did with his Chlorate Match. Then came the printed slip inserted inside the box of itself. This served a dual purpose — it helped to keep the matches from shaking about in the box (an important precaution because friction of matches against each other could easily cause them to ignite) and it also gave an extra publicity boost to the product; though people may not have bothered to read the box label their curiosity was usually aroused by a printed slip found inside. An illustration of this is the folded slip enclosed in every box of R. Bell & Co's Wired Fixed Stars — The Smoker's Friend. A crafty move, because natural curiosity means that a folded slip of paper is almost inevitably opened. And what did the purchasers of a box of Bell's Wired Fixed Stars read? 'YES SIR! These are the original and best WIRED FIXED STARS R. Bell & Co's Patent. Warranted not to drop the ash, being wired through the head into the wood. Ask for WIRED and have no others'. Although not the very early matches these are typical of the spate of improvements and refinements marketed in the 1850s and '60s.

On the really early labels advertising was muted. It was characterised by the elaborate scrollwork and fancy lettering beloved by the Victorians and was usually confined to publicising products of interest to smokers — tobacco, cigars etc. The manufacturers were obviously of the opinion that matches were bought mainly by smokers and so the advertising had to be aimed towards them; the housewife was ignored at that period.

Nearer the Edwardian era advertising became more imaginative. By the late 1800s 'customers' labels' were making their appearance. In Britain the canny northerners seemed to be the first to make use of such a promotion medium. You could buy a box of Cannan's Match with an eye-catching drawing of a cannon on the front and on the sides and back you could learn that 'The only Genuine Half-pound Penny pack of the BEST DRY SOAP is Cannan's'. Messrs Smith, Dixon and Lodge of Harper Street Chemical Works, Leeds, produced their 'no frills' Abbey Match, the front label being printed simply in black on off-

(first row) A nineteenth-century Swedish label. Was the fact that the head of a match never fell off really a triumph of science? It was hailed as such, as well as being a 'wonderfully interesting discovery'; Subtle advertising! This label was issued at a time when the Blue Ribbon temperance movement was strong in Edwardian Britain
(second row) An advertising label of a once busy industry which has long since died out
(third row) What strange cures the Victorians gave their children! A Swedish export label; Coates & Co's Black Friars Distillery is still making gin in Plymouth but these advertising labels were issued in the early part of this century
(fourth row) A gift coupon which doubled as a packet label for a dozen boxes of matches; An Edwardian label reveals what the well-dressed nurse wore at the time

A TRIUMPH of SCIENCE

RECOMMENDED BY ALL INSURANCE COMPANIES
AS A PROTECTION AGAINST FIRE

TEMPLE-BAR SPECIAL SAFETIES

ignite on the Box
the WOOD of EACH MATCH is

CHEMICALLY TREATED

So that the GLOWING Portion of wood NEVER FALLS off
(N.B. a fruitful CAUSE of disastrous & FATAL Fires)

TRY IT when the match is BLOWN OUT TRY IT
the wood CEASES to glow !!!
WONDERFULLY INTERESTING DISCOVERY

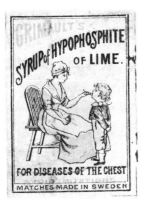

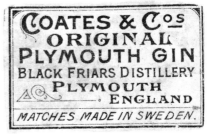

white paper with a picture of a ruined abbey. The side of the box read 'Dixon's Is the King of Baking Powders' and advised housewives that the powder was sold in 1d Packets; on the back panel was an inducement that no housewife could resist — 'NO MORE WASHING DAYS' and then in smaller type 'Should pass without using DIXON'S SOAP SUBSTITUTE'. Even in those days there were agile brains and smooth talkers in the advertising world! And where better to promote products than on something which the housewife was bound to use — a matchbox.

Modern advertising gimmicks for many products include coupons offering free gifts. We tend to regard this as a post World War II phenomenon but such ideas were first launched soon after the turn of the century and by 1913 Bryant & May was issuing coupons with the famous Puck and Captain Webb brands of strike-anywhere matches. In those days lighters had not superseded matches and lighting the gas was much more common than switching on the electricity, so people bought boxes of matches in dozen packs and got through them very quickly — they could afford to, since a dozen pack cost only 2d (just under 1p). The Puck and Captain Webb free gift coupons were printed on the dozen pack labels only. Whereas today one would probably require some thirty or so complete books of

(above left) Hardy's Butterfly Tea was probably a popular product in the early 1900s; *(centre left)* A pre World War I prize scheme to sell 'Zebra' matches; *(below)* A 1914 prize scheme run by Alsing Trading Co to promote 'Ship' matches

1920s all-round-the-box advertising labels for matches made in Flanders

trading stamps to obtain the 'gift' of one saucepan, with the Bryant & May offer one could become the proud possessor of no less than *thirty* enamel saucepans for 1,500 coupons, or, if you were a keep fit fanatic, you could trade in your coupons for a pair of dumb-bells. A clockwork toy or a rocking horse were popular coupon gifts as Christmas time approached, and the busy housewife could treat herself to a set of scrubbing brushes or a dustpan and brush if she used enough matches.

The scheme continued on a limited basis throughout World War I but was discontinued in 1918. However, in 1925 Bryant & May reintroduced it and widened the range of brands which it covered. It was still one coupon per twelve boxes of matches but in addition to Puck and Captain Webb matches coupons were also found on Ruby, Brymay, Pearl, Tiger, Bluebell and Pilot brands and to encourage people to buy even more

matches the prizes became more seductive. For instance, who could resist starting to save for a bedroom suite, even though 10,000 coupons were needed, and as an added enticement there was a three-monthly special prize awarded to the five people who sent in the highest number of coupons during the preceding three months. A 14/28 'Stratford' five-seater Standard motor car was the first prize, with a Triumph motor cycle and sidecar as second, an upright piano as third, an HMV cabinet gramophone (as much a status symbol then as video is today) as fourth and a BSA bicycle as fifth. Millions of coupons were sent in during the three years that the scheme ran. It was discontinued in June 1928 and Bryant & May has not run a gift coupons promotion since then.

In recent times Bryant & May has come up with some more very imaginative ideas to boost sales. By 1979 foreign imports of matches were

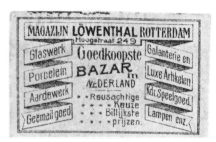

470, Bath Rd., Bristol 4,
Tel: 79654 & 78823

BASE LABEL FOR

Bouldens Match Company

Advertising Matches

AVERAGE CONTENTS 40 AUSTRIAN MATCHES

HON SEC. H. U. BATHE
11 OXFORD ST. SWINDON WILTS.
THE BRITISH MATCHBOX LABEL
AND BOOKLET SOCIETY

UNCLE MICK'S
MATCHES

*THE JUNIORS' CORNER
AT THE SOCIETY'S EXHIBITION
10th APRIL 1948*

threatening the British match industry and the
need for aggressive marketing techniques became
apparent. To sell matches and help a good cause
at the same time was one brainwave. On 3
January 1979 the Bryant & May 'Save a Swan'
campaign was launched, bringing together the
well known Swan Vestas brand and an appeal by
Sir Peter Scott, the world famous ornithologist,
to raise £10,000 for the protection and preservation of the handsome Bewick swan. This
threatened species is a winter migrant to Britain,
its principal habitat being the marshes of East
Anglia. In 1978 it was estimated that the world
population of Bewick swans had dropped to only
2,000 and the Wildfowl Trust was calling for
drastic action. Boxes of Swan Vestas matches
were printed with the slogan 'Save a Swan' and
inside each box was a tear-off tab, to be returned
to Bryant & May, which would donate one penny
to the Wildfowl Trust for every tab received. Also
Bryant & May produced a specially commissioned
print of Keith Shackleton's painting 'Bewick's
Swans through the Baltic' and for every print
purchased at £1.75 Bryant & May donated £25 to
the Wildfowl Trust.

In 1978 there appeared to be a swing back to
the use of matches in preference to lighters and
advertising was all important — such different
advertising from when Cannan's were promoting
their dry soap or Dixon's their soap substitute.

Two widely differing designs for modern Swiss advertising labels

The Belfast Evening Telegraph was the medium for
extensive advertising of a competition to win a
holiday in the USA, with details printed on
Bryant & May's two Northern Ireland brands,
Bo-Peep and Swift.

The lure of football was another brainwave in
1970s match promotion. J. John Masters was the
originator of this and organised a very successful
Treble Chance Match competition on its Vulcan
brand sold in Scotland. Vulcan sales increased by
10 per cent in three months and because of this
remarkable result Masters launched similar promotions nationally on its famous Ship brand and
also on Pioneer brand. This promotion involved

(first row) A very unexciting advertising label for a
Dutch department store in the 1920s; Not strictly an
advertising label but one which helped to promote
another product. This Indian label was a copy of the
famous Wills's Gold Flake cigarette packet of the
1930s, with the word 'Flake' altered to 'Flame' for the
match; A Hungarian advertising label for a brand of
washing powder sold in that country
(second row) A play on words for a soap firm's advertising label in the 1930s; The popular Bouldens'
advertising labels produced individually for each
customer *(centre)* are struck over a base label *(right)*
which advertises Bouldens itself
(third row) A privately printed advertising label for the
British Matchbox Label & Booklet Society. The late
Mr J. Michelson (shown in the photograph) who was
responsible for having the labels produced, looked after
the interests of the junior members of the society; A
late 1940s advertising label by the long defunct North
of England Match Co; Morelands relief on the English
love of cricket as an advertising gimmick for their
'England's Glory' matches

(left) A modern advertising label from Israel; *(right)*
Label advertising a store and a commemoration in 1975

A set of 1970s labels from Bulgaria advertising Balkan Tourist Authority holiday centres

shopkeepers as well, because every gross packet of boxes of matches contained a free entry form for the use of retailers in their own competition which offered the winner a Ford Fiesta car.

The appeal of a football promotion did not go unnoticed by other match firms and in the spring of 1979 Bryant & May introduced a tie-up with Ladbrooke's 'Spot the Ball' competitions. Entry forms were printed on boxes of matches and competitors could net a £40,000 prize if they were lucky.

Offers get more alluring and original with every new idea. Our grandparents would never have dreamt that a box of matches might bring them a holiday of a lifetime on an exotic Mediterranean island but that is possible in the 1980s, with J. John Masters' Vulcan Matches offering six prizes of two-week holidays in Crete and fifty prizes of eight-day holidays in Majorca — simply for producing an apt and original name for the famous ship which is the trade mark of Ship matches.

In the 1980s advertising on famous brands tended to change from the competition slant to the 'special offer', where the consumer is invited to send for various goods, ranging from a barbecue to a first-aid kit, obtainable at a lower than average price if the coupon on the matchbox is used.

Collectors will never be short of material now that advertising on matchbox labels has taken such a dramatic turn. Each new variety is something to be sought, bought or swapped, perhaps becoming a treasured rarity as it is superseded by a fresh subject.

With nothing new to offer in the way of matches themselves attention must be paid to gimmick promotions and packaging but in the latter field, again, the ways of presenting a matchbox are limited. However, the ingenuity of those in the advertising industry is boundless and in 1979 Bryant & May came up with Cook's Matches, presented in a rather unusual brown-coloured box. The pack still looked like a box of matches but the laminated surface of the outer cover could be wiped clean and kept free of grease spots in the kitchen. These matches were exten-

(left) Italian tomatoes advertised on a skillet for Spanish matches to be sold in Britain! *(centre)* A novel advertising skillet. The map of Australia is woven on material and stuck to the card to advertise the firm which specialises in that type of work; *(right)* One of Bryant & May's 'competition' skillets of the 1970s

sively advertised in women's magazines and went on the market at the price of 16p for a box of 280 sticks.

The 1970s saw a tremendous upsurge in the use of customer's labels' for boxes of matches sold in public houses, restaurants and so on. Firms which import and distribute the matches undertake to provide a personalised label for any establishment, often using a colour photograph of the bar or outside of the building and including the names of the licensees. Personalised advertising labels are used by all types of organisation from local clubs to churches selling matches as a way of raising cash towards their restoration funds. Such a one was the attractive pen and ink sketch of an ancient church reproduced on a plain white label, inscribed 'St Mary's, Ruabon'. These issues are, of course, strictly limited in number and their reception by collectors is mixed; some regard them as desirable because they are usually a small

'one off' issue, whereas others do not regard them as proper matchbox labels and will not bother to collect them.

Most countries have at one time or another used matchbox labels as an advertising medium. Some have been less restrained than others in the type of goods or services which they have advertised and the way in which they have presented their publicity.

To specialise in advertising labels is to take on a formidable task. For instance, in the 1930s Chinese manufacturers indulged in a spate of advertising of cigarettes, cosmetics, drinks etc on matchbox labels and the content of the advertisements changed so rapidly that it would be almost impossible to gather together anything like a complete collection covering only a few months.

Belgium, Holland, Finland and Czechoslovakia are a few of the European countries which for years have issued vast quantities of export

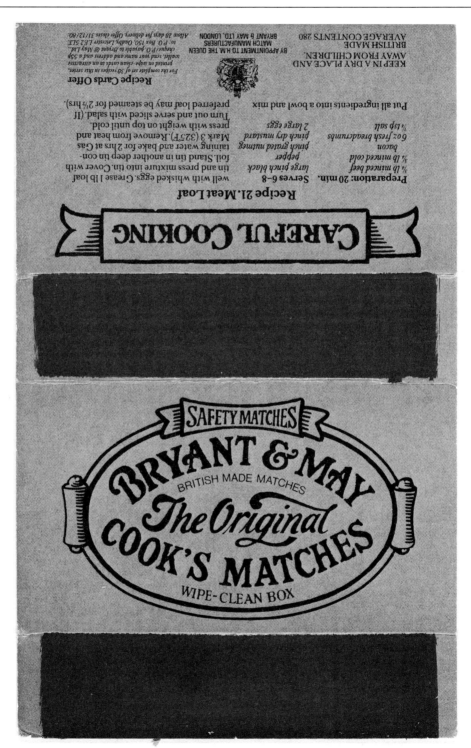

A constant striving after something new in matchbox design produced the wipe-clean box

(top) An advertising skillet of the 1980s from Eire; *(bottom)* A novel trend in modern advertising. This skillet features a magazine advertisement whilst at the same time selling the matches themselves by suggesting that one collects the complete set of matchboxes

labels promoting everything from margarine to cigars, and from coffee to underwear. In the 1930s Finland issued a great many matchbox labels for its home market, advertising films on current release. At the time of issue they were not particularly prized by collectors, now they form a group in which some people specialise and they are considered desirable items to have in a collection.

India, which has a quite large cottage industry in match manufacture, is another country which has used labels for advertising for many years and to a very large extent. Some of the offerings emanating from the cottage 'factories' are decidedly quaint and one wonders what sort of customer would accept such crudely drawn, worded and produced advertising material. Rubber stamps, torch batteries and wooden ploughs are just some of the things promoted on labels for home consumption in India.

The 1980s saw the appearance of the matchbox label that advertised the collecting of matchbox labels! Cigarette manufacturers Benson & Hedges issued a series of twelve skillets; on the front panel of the box is a full colour reproduction of one of the ultra-modern and sophisticated advertisements for Benson and Hedges cigarettes, which appeared in all the top magazines. The back panel of the box informs the purchaser that 'This matchbox features one of the award-winning advertisements that show the quality of Benson & Hedges King Size — Britain's biggest selling cigarette. It's one in a series of twelve. Why don't you collect them?' Surely the ultimate in advertising on matchbox labels and a far cry from G. F. Watts's leaflets.

6

THE DEVELOPING COUNTRIES

It is fascinating to see how developing countries have coped with the growth of their match industries. It is not possible to deal in detail with every country but a few wide-ranging examples will set the scene.

Take, for instance, Albania. This is, perhaps, Europe's forgotten country — at least as far as the west is concerned — and for years it was cut off completely, at its own wish. Because of the general air of national secrecy which covered (and still does cover to a certain extent) everything in the country, the early history of Albania's match industry is a closed book but at least we can go back to soon after World War I when Albania imported matches from Russia. Later it imported from Italy, Sweden and, it is believed, Austria, although there is no proof of the last being a supplier. During the Italian occupation after World War I SAFFA of Milan supplied matches to Albania; the matches were quite good quality, the labels neatly printed in black and red on white paper, giving at the top the name of the Albanian match monopoly and beneath that the national symbol of the Albanian eagle, and the contents figure. There were variations on this label and it was on all the boxes of matches used during the period of King Zog's reign.

After 1945, when Albania became a Russian satellite state, the country was encouraged to develop its own industries and efforts were made to renew home match production. It is thought that there had previously been attempts to start a match industry but no records or information are available. However, a factory was opened in the capital, Tirana, in a run-down building which later became a furniture store. One must assume that the production line was fairly primitive. The labels were the all-round-the-box type, crudely printed on very poor quality off-white paper.

There was no attempt to offer the consumer anything but a functional object — there was printing on the front of the label only and the back was left blank. The wording merely stated 'Shkrepsa' (matches), the address of the factory and the contents figure '50'. There were two variations — one printed in black, the other in dark green.

Albania is predominantly a tobacco-growing country and has several old-established tobacco factories. The match factory did not last for very long and when it closed down production was switched to the Partizani tobacco factory near Tirana, where match manufacture became a sideline to cigarette making. The whole operation appears to have been very unsophisticated. Both outer covers and trays were inexpertly made, apparently by hand. The box trays were of very thin cardboard, little more than thick paper, and were, in fact, often made of the printed card used for packing Partizani cigarettes in their very humble packets. The match splints were roughly made of poor quality wood and each match merely snapped off at the bottom. Match tips were unevenly coated and some had dark-brown composition whilst others had dark red or scarlet. From approximately 1954 Albania imported matches from Czechoslovakia and by 1957 production at the Partizani factory operated only intermittently, when supplies of imported matches ran out. The labels on the Albanian-made matchboxes were all propaganda types promoting among other things the country's agricultural production.

Travellers in the north of Albania during the 1950s and '60s were offered extraordinary packs of matches which must have harked back to the early days of match manufacture in Britain in the 1830s. These strange 'matchboxes' were actually packets of matches produced in the shape of the conventional bookmatch: the difference was that the Albanian products were made from paper of a cigarette packet type, with the matches, flat and only partially cut, being stuck haphazardly into a roughly cut strip of paper which was just folded over and stuck at the back with a dab of glue. Across the front was swished a brushful of inadequate striking abrasive and only about one in five of the matches in a pack would strike at all. There was no wording on the packets. They came in two varieties — one quite obviously handmade in what could charitably be described as a great hurry, the other slightly more presentable with marginally better quality paper and the appearance that the paper had been cut by some form of guillotine and the striking abrasive probably put on by some mechanical device. These oddities were on sale only in Shkoder, where they were produced. The slightly neater packs were manufactured in the tobacco factory, the other, more rough and ready ones, were assembled by workers in their homes, as a cottage industry.

In complete contrast matches imported from Bulgaria and sold in Tirana were good quality white poplar sticks in machine made boxes with well printed labels. Nowadays Albania still imports matches from Bulgaria and, since the political alignment of the country changed somewhat, also from China. The local industry never seems to have got off the ground to any great extent but progress is being made.

An example of a country successfully developing its own match industry comes from Cyprus. The island has had only two match factories, the first being started during World War II under the name of the Cyprus Match Factory Ltd and producing neat little wax matches in small size boxes. It was a good start but sadly the firm went bankrupt in 1950 when free import of matches was resumed and it could not compete with the supplies from the big match producing countries. But in 1964 the Aphrodite Match Co Ltd opened for business near Nicosia, in a modern factory with the most up-to-date machinery, good working conditions and even a model fire extinguisher system, deemed very necessary in such a fire-prone industry. The firm was encouraged and partially subsidised by the Cyprus government and its matches were also exported to several other countries.

There is a success story, too, for Nigeria, a Third World country which established its own

Mint Albanian labels printed on scrap paper *c*1955–6. Unlike many other countries, mint labels from Albania are extremely rare and practically unobtainable in or out of the country

(*first row*) Two labels announcing the independence of India (*left*) and Indonesia (*centre*); Pakistan came into the match manufacturing business after independence

(*second row*) At one time Sweden exported matches to French North Africa; Zambia's own early labels were simple in design

(*third row*) The former Indo-China had its own match factory when under French rule; Yugoslavia produced a label portraying an African ruler, to be sold on boxes of matches in his own province; The new Melanesian company in Papua New Guinea models its labels on Australian styles

match industry after it became independent in 1960. Prior to 1963 matches were always imported into Nigeria, the main suppliers being Sweden, Austria, Finland and in the latter years Hong Kong. Belgium and Britain also supplied matches from time to time. In 1963 the Match Company of Nigeria, which took the trade name Matchco, opened and in 1964 the Safety Match Manufacturing Co and the Star Match Co Ltd both opened their doors for business. All three factories were established in different parts of the vast country and from the start their products were quite good quality. Imports of matches were soon banned and the country became entirely self-sufficient in its match production, quite a feat in a comparatively short space of time. Civil war and a disastrous fire at one of the factories disrupted things to a certain extent but 'Made in Nigeria' matches and labels still conform to a high standard of quality, the labels being well designed to appeal to the local markets and well printed by modern methods. The number 'three' is superstitiously regarded as a good fortune number in Nigeria so it is not surprising that 'Three' figures prominently in the match label brands — Three Elephants, Three Minarets, Three Queens, Three Rings, Three Crests, Three Eagles and several more of the same type are all products of a thriving match industry.

Yet another country which it may be interesting to examine in the context of the development of its match industry is China. This is not so much a developing country as one which *has* developed, regressed, and is now developing all over again.

The making of matches in China commenced in the late nineteenth century and, meticulous and painstaking as the Chinese are, its first labels were neat and well printed, if simple in design. The original utilitarian decoration of beautifully inscribed characters detailing either the name of the brand or how to use the matches soon gave way to more colourful and more interesting designs portraying notable political or military figures or commemorating political or military events. The labels improved in quality and interest right up to the late 1920s. In the 1930s advertising fever hit China and matchbox labels were used to promote every conceivable product but mainly, as has been mentioned in Chapter 5, drinks, cigarettes, patent medicines and cosmetics. In the 1940s things changed dramatically. The Communist regime took over the

Cameroun and Uganda: two young countries in the world of match manufacture

match industry, the quality of paper and printing deteriorated and nothing but propaganda slogans and pictures adorned matchbox labels. These were, of course, all for home consumption. As the political scene within China changed so did the propaganda on its labels. With Mao Tse-tung in power almost every label carried quotations from his famous Little Red Book. Very few of these labels ever left the country and fortunate indeed is the collector outside China who can today boast of such specimens in his or her collection. Small match factories operating in the remote interior of the country churned out a quantity of labels printed on very thin paper and in some cases Maoist propaganda was combined with designs based on the old Chinese superstitions and religious beliefs, although all use of such material was officially banned. Presumably officialdom in remote provinces was not as strict as in the more densely populated and more accessible areas.

A bid for a share of the export market in countries sympathetic to the regime in China resulted in some not very well printed but quite colourful small labels bearing very unflattering portraits of the leaders of some East African and Middle East countries. As the regime settled down and a few western visitors began to trickle into the country an effort was made to produce matchbox labels

Several countries now produce 'parlour' size skillets

more acceptable to the outside world. The result was some most attractive sets of labels for the typical small Chinese boxes, depicting among other things charming Chinese 'wash paintings' or traditional subjects — the more romantic side of China which has been visualised by people in other countries. Some sets contained as many as 250 labels and it is extremely doubtful if any collector in the west has even one fully complete set. These labels were printed at the match factories in Shanghai and Peking and were available to foreign visitors. In the hinterland the match industry continued more or less to stagnate, with appalling shortages of matches at times and rough and ready labels on those boxes which were available.

Since the end of the so-called Cultural Revolution something of a revolution has taken place in China's match industry. It has to a large extent been redeveloped. By 1972 American influence was being felt and the skillet put in its first appearance in China. Now all the large hotels and restaurants which cater for tourists sell beautifully printed and colourful skillets as well as pretty little boxes of matches carrying labels produced in the latest foil method of printing. These depict everything from pictures of an hotel to reproductions of Chinese works of art and scenes from Chinese folklore. Even in Mao's time the panda was a popular label subject — it still is, only printed on better quality paper and embellished now with foil decoration to add glamour. The collecting of matchbox labels, like the match industry, has been born again in China and apparently enthusiasm is running high. There is said to be a black market in the labels and booklets produced in the 200 state monopoly match factories throughout China, with unscrupulous

dealers charging exorbitant prices for mint sets. It is even said that sets of Chinese labels are peddled by shady characters on the streets of Hong Kong.

There is a tendency towards thinking that only the largest, the wealthiest or the most advanced countries have an efficient match industry and that elsewhere it is merely a cottage or makeshift industry with none of the modern refinements. However, this is not the case at all. Singapore can be taken as a random example. In 1967 the Federal Match Co Ltd, a joint venture between British and local interests, opened its modern factory with a staff of eighty people trained to operate some of the most modern matchmaking and packing equipment in the world. The matchboxes are made, labelled, filled and packed automatically; likewise the 'tipping' of the match with the chemical composition and the side coating of the boxes with the abrasive 'paint' on which the matches are struck. Nothing could be further from the image of the unskilled worker painstakingly filling each box of matches by hand and painting the striking surface on the box with a paintbrush. Although match manufacturing continues to a certain extent as a cottage industry in India, even there modern methods are gradually coming into use and much of the drudgery is being taken out of matchmaking.

There are not many countries which do not today produce their own matches — could Iceland be the only exception? As far as I know Iceland still imports all its matches and no label album has a section marked 'Iceland'. As far as the developing countries are concerned most of them have started up a match industry of sorts, to tie in with their image of independence and self sufficiency.

7

MODERN TRENDS

One may think that the collecting of matchbox labels has always been much the same, that people always seek and save the same things, and that a collection formed in the 1920s or earlier must cover similar trends to one formed today.

This is not the case at all. As with most things, collecting habits are progressive and there are fashions in collecting labels, just as there are in antiques. At the present time one of the main preoccupations of the younger generation of collectors is gathering what are generally known as 'pub' labels, produced by or for various inns from the tiny village free house to the vast chains of elaborate hostelries run by the large brewery combines.

A few years ago it was the seemingly interminable Whitbread set that held the stage. The Whitbread Wessex Inns set was advertised as 'A striking collection of matchboxes depicting 900 Whitbread inns' and Whitbread claimed that it was the largest series ever issued. The labels show full colour photographs of either the exteriors of the inns or the inn signs. Whitbread issued a beautifully produced album-type holder for its collection, the only snag being that each album had spaces for only 36 of the 900 labels, so 25 albums were needed if one was fortunate enough to gather the complete set. At the time of writing I have not come across anyone who possesses the full set, although quite a number of collectors count the labels in their collections in hundreds.

One good idea breeds others and imitations soon spring up, so it was not long before the St George's Taverns Famous Inn Signs set was available to customers. Collectors who never frequent pubs are still clamouring to obtain the colourful labels which made up the set of fifty. The St George's Taverns chain offered an attractive album with the added inducement of twelve

labels already mounted to start off the collection. Other St George's Taverns Inn Signs sets have followed the original one and examples are eagerly bought and exchanged.

The Wessex Taverns set of inn signs produced by the Cornish Match Company is another popular recent set although much shorter in length than the others. Joshua Tetley & Son, brewers of Tetley Ales, issued an attractive set of twenty-four skillets depicting Tetley Inn Signs in full colour. The printing of 'Series A' on the skillets indicates that another set is to come. As Tetley Inns are in the north of England the set must be regarded as very much a regional one.

Very much in demand by collectors following this modern trend is the elegant set of skillets issued for Schooner Inns. These featured pen-and-ink type sketches of the various pubs in the chain and it is believed that at least 135 different ones were issued. The set was comparatively short lived because Schooner Inns were taken over by Berni Inns and the set of matchboxes were discontinued.

Perhaps of the greatest interest to pub label collectors are the familiarly-called 'Bouldens'. The name comes from a firm, based in the south of England, which supplies personal advertising boxes of matches to pubs, organisations and individuals all over the country. The firm, which imports matches from Austria, Finland, Belgium etc, undertakes to design a label specially to the requirements of the customer. Of course many of these are local issues in the narrowest sense: pubs can have a colour photograph of the exterior of

(*opposite*) At one time, as much as possible in text and illustration was crammed onto a matchbox label

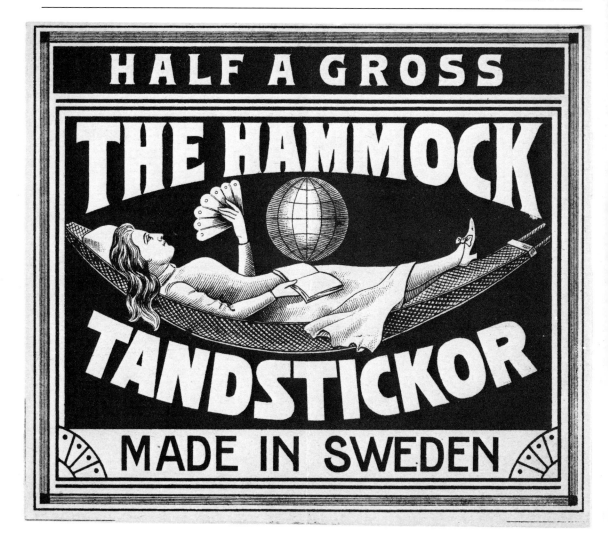

An old Swedish label from a half-gross packet of boxes
of matches

(opposite)
(top) Nineteenth-century advertising on matchboxes
was, to say the least, extravagant. This is an all-round-
the-box label for a longitudinal box; *(centre left)* A
modern advertising label which encourages collectors
to try and complete the set, thus ensuring a good sale
for Spar Stores' own brand of matches and *(below)*
Switzerland cleverly promotes some of its most famous
tourist attractions on a label which is not supposed to
be an advertising label at all; *(centre right)* A modern
advertising skillet. Boxes of these matches were given
away to purchasers of Clan Tobacco; *(bottom left to
right)* A mint Albanian label c1955–6; Sweden
exported matches to French North Africa at one time;
Nigeria announces its independance through this
matchbox label; Mali a 'young' country in the world of
match manufacture

LEWIS'S

GREAT TAILORING ESTABLISHMENT IS THE LARGEST IN * ENGLAND *

MATCHES MADE IN BELGIUM

LEWIS'S

MENS AND BOYS CLOTHING · IS THE BEST IN * ENGLAND *

THIS IS LEWIS'S WONDERFUL PENNY BOX OF MATCHES

LEWIS'S is unlike any other HOUSE of BUSINESS, the profit put on every Article is smaller than any SHOPKEEPER would be satisfied with. If ANY PERSON DOUBTS THIS TRUTH, let him buy in twelve different DEPARTMENTS at LEWIS'S a dozen different articles indiscriminately. LET HIM TAKE THEM AWAY and if he finds at the end of a week that any of the ARTICLES can be bought as cheaply at any other SHOP or WARE-HOUSE LEWIS'S will take back the articles in question and return the money.

LEWIS'S great establishment in Ranelagh Street, LIVERPOOL.

SPAR

MADE IN U.S.S.R.

FLAGS OF COUNTRIES WITH SPAR STORES- No1 of a series HOLLAND

AVERAGE 30 MATCHES

überall entzündbar s'allument partout

Tourist ZÜNDHÖLZER

TRUSTFREIE ZÜNDWARENFABRIK/KANDERGRUND A.G.

Clan NIEMEYER MIXTURE ®

WITH THE COMPLIMENTS OF THE AROMATIC PIPE TOBACCO.

Average contents 32 matches.

Made in Japan.

PIPEMEN'S LONG MATCHES

Special Clan Matches for the pipe smoker burn longer than standard matches. So now it's easier to perfect the art of lighting your pipe, without burning your fingers. And the long splints are excellent for cleaning your pipe bowl.

SIGURONI KULTURAT BUJQESORE dhe GJENE E GJALLE

TUNISIE

CONTRIBUTIONS INDIRECTES

MADE IN SWEDEN

INDEPENDANT NIGERIA 1960

FABRIQUE D'ALLUMETTES ECLAIR DANSEUR DOGON RÉPUBLIQUE DU MALI

ALLUMETTES DE SURETE

THE CHINAMAN

SAFETY MATCHES
MADE IN SWEDEN

SAFETY MATCH

AKAMATSU SEIZO

THE CHINAMAN

SAFETY MATCHES
MADE IN SWEDEN.

CUNARD

CLOSE COVER BEFORE STRIKING

Hamilton Taverns

White Horse

WHITE HORSE, NORTHAMPTON
SERIES OF 18 No 1

Wessex Taverns   No 1

The
Rowden Arms

ROWDEN ARMS
Rowden Hill, Chippenham, Wiltshire.
For Restaurant Tel: (0249) 3870

THE MARRIAGE OF THE PRINCE OF WALES AND
LADY DIANA SPENCER ~ WEDNESDAY 29 JULY 1981

E2994   Redheads
CONTENTS 47 MATCHES
MADE IN AUSTRALIA. BRYANT & MAY

REPÚBLICA DEL PERÚ

CORTESÍA DE LA
COMPAÑÍA SUECA DE FÓSFOROS

THE
ROYAL WEDDING

On 29th July 1981
The Nation Rejoices
The Cornish Match Co Ltd 48 Finnish Sticks

SOUTHERN COUNTIES MATCH CO. POOLE

H.R.H. PRINCE CHARLES   AND   LADY DIANA SPENCER

Royal Wedding

Average 40 Swiss Matches

1906 FRANKLIN

©1977 OHIO MATCH COMPANY
WADSWORTH, OHIO U.S.A. 44281

Lightweight at 1400 lbs.
Featured a 4-cyl, air cooled
engine. Saved about 200
lbs. without water cooling
apparatus. Sold for $1800.

FRANKLIN
1906

CLOSE COVER BEFORE STRIKING

КРАЉЕВИНА ЈУГОСЛАВИЈА

KRALJEVINA JUGOSLAVIJA

SVENSKA TANDSTICKS AKTIEBOLAGET

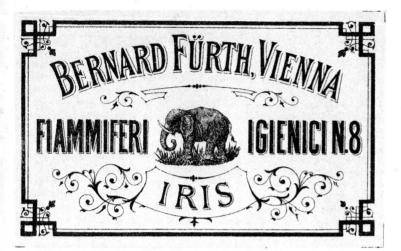

REPUBLICA DEL ECUADOR

MONOPOLIO DEL ESTADO

Profiad yw'r athro gorau :
trwy brofiad dysgwn lawer
o bethau nad ydym am eu
dysgu. —*W/102*

AVERAGE CONTENTS 48 · PRICE 2½d

(*top left*) In the nineteenth century Austrian matches were exported to Italy; (*top right*) 'England's Glory' matches for sale in Wales only carried quotations and jokes printed in Welsh; (*bottom left*) At one time, Sweden had the monopoly of providing 'official' labels for many different countries. These were used in government offices, official residences and the like; (*bottom centre*) Bryant & May had labels printed in German

(*opposite*)
(*first row*) The Chinaman, a popular brand at the turn of the century; A Cunard bookmatch cover of a type once sold on board *Queen Mary*
(*second row*) Two pub labels, now very popular with younger collectors; The Queen Mother featured on one of a set of labels issued in Australia to mark the Royal Wedding in 1981
(*third row*) A Swedish-made label for Peruvian government use; A straightforward Royal Wedding commemorative label of 1981; One of a modern American set of bookmatches featuring old cars
(*fourth row*) A pre-war Yugoslavian official label; A particularly attractive label to celebrate the Wedding of Prince Charles to Lady Diana Spencer; (*centre bottom*) Another Swedish label for foreign government use

An uncut sheet of a set of recent pictorial labels. Subjects in such sets range from views of buildings and beauty spots to portraits of footballers, pictures of tropical fish, locomotives, cars, dogs and many other subjects

CHATEAUX OF BORDEAUX

Series of 12. No. 1. CHATEAU BEAUREGARD
In the Pomerol District of Bordeaux.

CHATEAUX OF BORDEAUX

Series of 12. No. 2. CHATEAU GAZIN
In the Pomerol District of Bordeaux.

CHATEAUX OF BORDEAUX

Series of 12. No. 3. CHATEAU MALESCOT ST. EXUPERY
In the Margaux District of Bordeaux.

CHATEAUX OF BORDEAUX

Series of 12. No. 4. CHATEAU LA TOUR MARTILLAC
In the Graves District of Bordeaux.

CHATEAUX OF BORDEAUX

Series of 12. No. 5. CHATEAU HAUT BRION
In the Graves District of Bordeaux.

CHATEAUX OF BORDEAUX

Series of 12. No. 6. CHATEAU MARGAUX
In the Margaux District of Bordeaux.

CHATEAUX OF BORDEAUX

Series of 12. No. 7. CHATEAU BEYCHEVELLE
In the St. Julien District of Bordeaux.

CHATEAUX OF BORDEAUX

Series of 12. No. 8. CHATEAU COS d'ESTOURNEL
In the St. Estephe District of Bordeaux.

CHATEAUX OF BORDEAUX

Series of 12. No. 9. CHATEAU CLERC-MILON
In the Pauillac District of Bordeaux.

CHATEAUX OF BORDEAUX

Series of 12. No. 10. CHATEAU LYNCH-BAGES
In the Pauillac District of Bordeaux.

CHATEAUX OF BORDEAUX

Series of 12. No. 11. CHATEAU MOUTON-BARON-PHILIPPE
In the Pauillac District of Bordeaux.

CHATEAUX OF BORDEAUX

Series of 12. No. 12. CHATEAU PICHON-LONGUEVILLE, COMPTESSE DE LALANDE
In the Pauillac District of Bordeaux.

(opposite) Two early twentieth-century wrapper labels for packets of one dozen boxes of matches. Variation in colour of paper and printing create important variations for collectors

INN SIGNS No. 12

LAMB & FLAG
(See also No. 27)

HEMELING
Lite LAGER

AVERAGE 48 MATCHES · MADE IN BELGIUM

The Red Lion Hotel

Prop. Mr. M.C. MAIDMENT

Tel: SALISBURY 23334

SALISBURY · ENGLAND

St. George's Taverns Inn Signs

Series of 50. No. 9

Average Contents 40. Made in Finland

PETER BOAT
High Street,
Leigh-on-Sea, Essex.

THE HALFWAY HOTEL
Tel: Parkstone 741463

4p

Discotheque/Skittle Alley

Badger Beer/Accommodation

The Cornish Match Co. Ltd., St. Ives, Cornwall

Speciality Made by

Courage (Western) Ltd.

17 87

**JOHN COURAGE
STRONG PALE ALE**

Average Contents 50 Finnish Sticks

North
Country
Beer

AVERAGE 52 CONTENTS

FOREIGN MAKE

**DOUBLE
DIAMOND**

WORKS WONDERS !

THE
BRITISH
INN

AVERAGE 30 FOREIGN MATCHES

Average 40 matches   2p   Made in Belgium

(above and opposite) Some of the modern 'pub' and brewery skillets and labels so popular with younger collectors and others who have taken up the hobby in recent years

FOR GOOD FOOD AND DRINK

2ᴰ 2ᴰ

AVERAGE 30

FOREIGN MATCHES

St GEORGE'S TAVERNS

COMPANY BROCHURES AVAILABLE AT EVERY HOUSE

Matchmakers Ltd, Hayes, Middx. / A.V.- 40   MADE IN SPAIN

For M&B Brew XI

Schooner Inns

Schooner Inns

THE CORNISH MATCH CO. LTD ST IVES, CORNWALL

THE TREGUTH INN, HOLYWELL BAY, Nr. NEWQUAY, CORNWALL.

THE PLYMOUTH BREWERIES LIMITED

Nun's

1879 ++++++ 1979

Centenary

NUNEATON RUGBY FOOTBALL CLUB

AV. CONTENTS 45 ASPEN STICKS

PTB SUPERKEG

EXTRA LONG AUSTRIAN MATCHES

PLYMOUTH AND TORQUAY

THE ELDON, NEWCASTLE.

A'la Carte Restaurant

PPP LTD LEICESTER 0533 432222

AV. CONT 45 AUSTRIAN MATCHES

THE ROYAL, HORSEBRIDGE, DEVON
Accommodation, Bar Meals – Tel: Milton Abbot 214

THE DOLPHIN

AK

Marian & Morton
welcome you
91 Railway St.
Hertford

Tel: Hertford 52944

A Mac's House

Matchmakers Ltd, Hayes, Middx./ A.V.-40   MADE IN SPAIN

3

THE DOLPHIN

AVERAGE 48 MATCHES

Ram Rod
STRONG BOTTLED
BITTER

CZECHOSLOVAK MAKE

Warwick
Castle

Warwick Place W.9
286·9604

NORMAN & JULIE DYER

DIAMOND INTERNATIONAL CORP., DIAMOND MATCH DIVISION, NEW YORK, N.Y. 10017

diamond ◆ KITCHEN MATCHES

American Revolution Bicentennial 1776-1976

diamond KITCHEN MATCHES

diamond ◆ KITCHEN MATCHES

 DIAMOND INTERNATIONAL CORP., DIAMOND MATCH DIVISION, NEW YORK, N.Y. 10017

MADE IN U.S.A.

STRIKE **diamond** ANYWHERE

KITCHEN
MATCHES

CONTENTS: 250 MATCHES

DE GAMLA ETIKETTERNA.

Tidigare har utkommit:
Serie 1, 1978, 22 motiv
Jub. serie 1978, 22 motiv
Serie 1, 1979, 15 motiv
Serie 2, 1979, 15 motiv
Spec. serien 1979, 15 motiv
Serie 1, 1980, 15 motiv
Serie 2, 1980, 15 motiv
Specialserien 1980, 15 motiv

Solstickan (1 öre/ask)
AB Jönköping-Vulcan

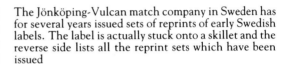

Ser 1 nr 13 1981

The Jönköping-Vulcan match company in Sweden has for several years issued sets of reprints of early Swedish labels. The label is actually stuck onto a skillet and the reverse side lists all the reprint sets which have been issued

the building, a view of the bar or other internal features, or a picture of the landlord and his wife behind the bar, plus advertising text of their choice. The numbers issued must far exceed even Whitbread's famous 900 and it is most unlikely that anyone will ever be able to track down every Boulden's label. Some collectors specialise in Bouldens alone and will travel miles to visit a pub which has its own Boulden's label.

Some rather amusing misprints have crept into these modern labels. The Schooner Inn skillets, for all their sophisticated appearance and well produced artwork, had some curious mistakes on them. The skillet for The Old Sugar Loaf at Dunstable had the name of the hostelry printed as 'The Old Sugar Leaf', The Wig and Gown at Maidstone appeared as 'The Wig and Crown' and The Whyte Lyon, Hartley Wintney as 'The White Lyon, Hartley, Wintney', whilst a St George's Taverns Inn Signs label for Chequers, Isleworth, had printed at the top 'Series of 16, No. 54'! This is the sort of thing that the keen-eyed collector is always trying to spot.

It must, however, be understood that misprints on matchbox labels do not instantly make them more valuable, as happens with postage stamps. Nor does the wrong use of one word for another make a matchbox label soar in value, since this happened quite frequently on early Japanese labels and still sometimes happens on labels printed in English in a foreign country. Such

things are merely amusing novelties to the collector.

Another characteristic of the modern trend in collecting in Britain is the accumulation of the numerous sets of labels which are now issued almost solely with collectors in mind. A decade or so ago sets such as these were virtually unknown. True there have in the past been sets of matchbox labels such as J. John Masters' Rank Markings of the Services and the popular Punch Lines on the Punch all-round-the-box labels but the multi-coloured sets of views, cars, fish, dogs and locomotives, to name but a few, were yet to come. Now they come in such abundance on boxes of matches imported from foreign countries that many serious collectors and those of the older generation spurn them altogether. Such sets are colourful and attractive, appealing to the collecting instinct but hardly likely to be the great rarities or classics of the future.

Yet another feature for the label collector which has put in an appearance in comparatively recent years, starting on the continent and spreading to Britain, is the souvenir or tourist pack of matchboxes. These, produced *solely* with the collector or souvenir-hunter in mind, comprise a set of matchboxes (usually skillets) wrapped in cellophane packs of five, six or ten or whatever number of boxes the distributors choose and are usually found in seaside resorts, tourist

(opposite) The United States of America remembers the American Revolution

haunts and large cities. These range from sets of local views to packs of 'Funnies' — plastic matchboxes bearing vulgar or suggestive drawings or jokes and more likely to be found on sale in London or other large cities than in, perhaps, the fishing villages of Cornwall. Again, serious and/or long-standing collectors do not rush to obtain such items but to newer and younger collectors they are quite the thing to have in a collection.

This, then, is the way that the hobby of collecting matchbox labels is going today. There will always be the enthusiasts who take pleasure in building up the accepted concept of a classic collection, seeking the old, the rare and the unusual, and alongside them are the modern generation of collectors seeking what the purists regard as rubbish but which gives just as much pleasure to those interested in it.

The collecting of matchbox labels or match-related items is essentially a 'do your own thing' hobby — long may it remain so!

8

KNOW YOUR LABELS

The author who has the temerity to suggest how one should go about forming a matchbox label collection is really sticking out his or her neck, but personal experience must be the peg on which all advice is hung and readers can experiment around that to their heart's delight.

The vast majority of collectors keep labels soaked off from the wooden or cardboard outer covers of the boxes; a few collect labels 'on wood' only (a guarantee that they are genuine and not just printed as collectors' items) and some like complete boxes, either empty or with original full complement of matches. In the latter case storage space and fire risk are both points to be considered. House insurance may well be affected if the dwelling contains large quantities of unused matches and storage can be a problem in many modern houses, where space is at a premium. A large collection of labels mounted in a great many albums takes up a lot of room and anything more bulky than that should be carefully considered before deciding on the form a collection is to take.

It is generally accepted that matchbox labels are best housed in loose-leaf albums. A collection of this kind is constantly growing and so there is always the need for more pages to be added, for labels to be moved around and for easy access to all items. Naturally, the choice of an album must be a matter of personal preference but it is wise to settle for a standard line supplied by a firm which is not likely to go out of business. That way continuity can be kept — all albums will be the same size; the same colour, if desired; and will always look neat and tidy in whatever form of storage is chosen or available. There is nothing more annoying than starting a collection in one type of album, whether elaborate or simple, only to find, as the collection grows and another album is

needed, that the original type is no longer available. For those who can afford to commission made-to-measure albums there is no problem, but the average collector usually prefers to spend hobby money on increasing the size and quality of his or her collection rather than on costly albums. There are collections in existence which are housed not only in specially made albums but also in specially made bookcases, but that is the exception to the rule.

For my own part I have always kept my collection in simple ring binders filled with lined paper. Such albums are always available from stationers, they are comparatively cheap, offer exceptional ease of movement for sheets, which can be taken out or put in at will, and are a neat and tidy way of keeping a collection. Even for the youngest beginner they are far more satisfactory than an ordinary exercise book and not much more expensive, especially if one watches out for the bargain offers on such articles run from time to time by the chain stationers such as W. H. Smith.

Whatever type of album is chosen the golden rule is that labels must *never* be stuck down to the paper. Countless early and potentially valuable collections have been ruined because the labels were stuck with glue or other adhesive to the album pages. Even modern adhesives which are 'peelable' should never be used. Labels must *always* be fixed to album pages by stamp hinges and it is sensible to buy the best quality available, so that they will peel easily from both label and page without leaving marks on either. Never be tempted to make your own hinges from a roll of adhesive tape such as sellotape. This in time discolours and can badly mark labels as the stain usually works through to the front, leaving an ugly mark which cannot be removed and which could render a rare label valueless.

An early twentieth-century wrapper for a dozen boxes of matches

The removal of the label from the wood or cardboard outer cover has long been a bone of contention among collectors — everybody has a favourite way of 'soaking off' and everybody thinks that way is the best. It is largely a matter of trial and error to find the method best suited to *your* requirements. Over forty-seven years of collecting I have tried just about every method recommended but for many years have stayed with the immersion-in-boiling-water treatment and have always found it satisfactory. Other methods have sometimes proved disastrous although perhaps recommended by other collectors.

The immersion-in-boiling-water method is just what it says — the label, still adhering to wood or cardboard, is totally immersed in boiling water. After an appropriate length of time, it can be removed easily and is blotted between clean blotting paper (or even newspaper for very common and not at all valuable labels) before being laid out to dry naturally in the air. Admittedly, this method has its dangers and one has to be vigilant; it is no good tipping a whole lot of box tops or outer covers into a bowl of boiling water and just leaving them until you have the time or inclination to remove them. Every label must be treated individually; you can put several labels at one time into the water but care must be taken when soaking off in bulk because types of adhesive, quality of wood or cardboard, thickness of the paper label etc vary considerably, especially between countries, and some labels can be ruined if soaked indiscriminately.

Modern Australian labels, which come in many attractive sets and are popular with collectors because of the fun of working to complete the sets, will serve to illustrate the point. Australian matchboxes are often made of blue cardboard and this poses terrible problems when soaking off the labels; the blue will often stain the back of the label when it is put into hot water and instead of a white background label one ends up with a blue background one which *cannot* be passed off as a different variety! The secret here is speed of removal from the card. Have the water really boiling and pop the labels in and out very quickly, before the blue dye has time to permeate them. It can be done and is the method I always employ in dealing with such labels. Experience will show you how long to leave a label of this type in the water but the type of adhesive used for the labels

usually dissolves very quickly and a few seconds immersion is all that is needed.

Another problem which irks collectors is that some countries stain the edges of wooden outer covers to preserve them. Magenta and yellow are the favourite colours for this practice and as soon as the labels on wood go into the boiling water the dye starts seeping into the paper. Again, speed and constant watching are essential: once you have put the wooden top in the water watch it intently and as soon as the label shows signs of floating off, whip it out of the water and peel off the label immediately; the same applies if there is any suggestion of the dye running—it will colour both the water and the label. There are certain solvents which can be used for removing problem labels of this type: the solvent is applied over the label and as it soaks through it removes the label from the wood. I have never been over-enamoured of this method and have found that although the label seems all right when removed from the wood it does in time tend to rot or become discoloured and eventually a better specimen has to be substituted in the album. That is all very well with common labels but is often not possible with rare varieties.

Before being mounted the label should be completely free of any extraneous material such as strips of backing paper; this should be carefully peeled or scraped off when the label is removed from the cover. Some foreign manufacturers use thick, cloying glue to affix labels to outer covers and this means that when the label has been soaked off it still has a thin film of glue on its back. If left this film of glue will cause the label to crinkle as it dries, so all traces should be very carefully scraped off with a small penknife or similar instrument.

All this applies to simple labels affixed on the top or bottom of a box but there are such things as all-round-the-box labels (usually referred to by collectors as ARTBs). The same rules apply to them although they are a little more tricky to remove. An all-round-the-box label should *never* be cut. It is a great temptation, especially when one is a beginner trying to build up a stock of labels for exchanging, to make an all-round label into two by cutting the front and back panels. This immediately ruins and renders completely valueless any all-round label and should never be done. Most collectors will not accept cut labels for exchange, anyway, so instead of gaining an

BRYANT & MAY'S NAME and
TRADE MARK
SECURITY
Appear upon Every Box
and also upon Every
dozen Packet
BY ROYAL LETTERS PATENT
FRAUD
PROTECTION FROM FIRE
BRYANT & MAY Patentees & only Manufacturers of the Special Safety Match Wax Vesta and Vesuvian which contain no Phosphorus and ignite on the prepared surface of the box. The Prize Medal for these Safety Lights was awarded to BRYANT AND MAY at the Great Exhibition of all Nations 1862.
FAIRFIELD WORKS, BOW, LONDON.
PROTECTION FROM FIRE
ROYAL
PATENT
SECURITY
BRYANT & MAY'S
SPECIAL SAFETY MATCH
IS NOT POISONOUS
1862
LONDINI
HONORIS
CAUSA
THESE
SPECIAL MATCHES
Have been before the BRITISH PUBLIC for 35 Years.

SEE OVER

An early, double-sided advertising leaflet issued by Bryant & May

extra label you are left with two worthless bits of paper. All-round labels must always be removed in one piece, starting from the join which is usually on the top or side of the box. Here, again, a small penknife is very handy for lifting the corner of the label which, if it has been soaked long enough, should peel off easily in one piece. Special care must be taken to ease it off gently at the folds around the cover.

If an extra piece of striking abrasive has been stuck on separately over the label itself (often the case with stike-anywhere matches) that can be carefully peeled off before the label is removed from the cover. Composition for striking safety matches can cause ugly marks on the opposite page when the label is mounted in an album. This can be avoided to a large extent if the abrasive is brushed off when thoroughly wet with an old, soft toothbrush before the label is peeled from the cover. Beware rubbing too hard, it is easy to rub a hole in the paper and it is seldom possible to remove all traces of striking material anyway.

Nowadays an increasing number of matchbox outer covers are skillets, that is cardboard outers onto which the design is printed. They are not too popular with some collectors but it is a trend which has to faced and if one does not collect skillets one is undoubtedly going to miss a lot of interesting issues. There is no getting away from the fact that skillets are bulky to store and difficult to mount satisfactorily in albums as when mounted they make the pages bulge unpleasantly. The answer is that one does not mount the whole thickness; the skillet can be 'thinned' and with practice this is quite a simple operation.

The card of which skillets are made is built up in layers and again the boiling water treatment is desirable. Immerse the whole outer cover in the water and soon the adhesive which joins it will dissolve and it will most likely pop open. If it does not open of its own accord it can be very gently forced. Once it is open the adhesive which held it together must be carefully scraped off with a penknife or something similar and the by now flat cover put back in the water again. Leave it for a little longer than you would an ordinary label and when it appears to be thoroughly soaked you can start peeling off the layers of card. Start at the corner and peel back very carefully; if the first layer does not come off easily it has not been soaked for long enough and should be put back into the water for a short while. The top layer,

which is what is wanted, usually comes off fairly easily as a complete label and is treated the same way as a label before being mounted in the album. A little skill is required to perfect the technique of thinning skillets and it is wise to practice first on some which you do not mind spoiling.

Though soaking in boiling water is suitable for the vast majority of labels and skillets a word of warning must be made concerning the exceptions. These are usually really old labels. In Victorian times it was common for labels to be printed in mauve, purple or light magenta. These are 'fugitive' colours and will not only fade if exposed for long periods to daylight, and especially sunlight, but will fade or run if immersed in hot water. Very early labels can also be extremely fragile and it is most unwise to subject anything in this line to the water treatment. If the labels come to you on wood it is advisable to keep them that way and mount them in the album wood and all. Complete boxes should, of course, be left intact. Warm, not boiling water, will not harm some early labels but it means that they must be left in the water for a longer period and watched constantly for any signs of deterioration. Needless to say, the peeling process has to be carried out *very* carefully. If in any doubt about how a label will stand the soaking, don't use it.

Having accumulated a selection of labels the collector must decide how they should be classified in the album. By far the most popular method is by country of origin, with a special 'Don't Know' section at the back of the album in which to put any unidentified labels. This is usually regarded as a temporary measure because sooner or later you are sure to find out their country of origin and can then move them to their rightful place. Labels in this section are usually marked 'Foreign Made' or 'Foreign Make' or even just 'Foreign' or do not have any indication at all of their origin.

Most people start collecting on a worldwide basis, keeping anything and everything which comes their way, and their collection soon grows. There may, however, come a point where a collection gets too unwieldly in this format and then a decision is often taken to specialise. The scope for specialisation is almost endless: it is entirely a matter of personal preference. Single countries or groups of countries are popular. If choosing a single country make sure that it is one which has issued plenty of labels. To specialise in just Great

Britain or Sweden or Belgium for instance would be all right but to choose, say, Albania or Nicaragua might be difficult because not only has their output been small but the labels are also extremely difficult to obtain. So if your interest leans towards such areas it would be better to go in for a group of countries — Central America, Southern Europe, South America etc.

Thematic collecting, that is under subject matter, is also popular and here again a little thought is necessary before a decision is taken. Anyone specialising in labels depicting elephants would find plenty of labels available to fill an album but to choose labels showing perhaps llamas or giraffes would be very restricting because so few issues depict these animals. It would be better to go for a broad heading such as animals or transport or royalty — the last two are particularly favoured subjects.

Thematic collecting can pose some very tricky problems. For example, you may have sections in your album for transport, animals, people, mythology, flora, fauna and so on, and at first it seems very straightforward. But sooner or later you are going to come across perhaps a Japanese label showing a lady riding in a horse-drawn vehicle and brandishing a large flower. So how do you classify that? Should it come under transport, or people, or flora or fauna? A difficult decision to make and it could crop up time and again, so be warned before you decide to arrange your collection on a strictly thematic basis.

In addition to single and all-round labels and skillets there are other types which, though not common, are still matchbox labels and have their place in a collection. These are pill box and banderole labels. The pill box is a small circular label affixed to the top of the lid of a cylindrical cardboard box which usually contains wax matches. Such matchboxes are, or have been, particularly popular in Australia and New Zealand; in more recent times these have also come from Italy in the form of decorative cylinders usually put on sale around Christmas time. The banderole is a long narrow streamer which wraps around a cylindrical box and was mainly used in Austria and Germany at the turn of the century. Strip labels are also used in some countries to seal over the end flaps of boxes.

The term 'skillet' can be applied to the springflap boxes which are so common in Italy and some other countries and these should be treated as skillets when being prepared flat for the album. They will, however, open out with side flaps and care must be taken that small bits such as tabs are not torn off when the outer cover of a springflap box is opened.

We have up to now talked only about box labels but there is another type which appeals to some collectors. This is the 'big boy' — the gross and dozen size label, used on the bulk packets supplied to the retailer and on the dozen (or now tens) packs of matches which the retailer sells to the public. These are soaked from their paper and mounted in albums in the same way as box labels but they do take up a lot of room and many people prefer not to collect them, although they do occasionally present desirable features which are not on the box labels. An example is the 1955 Blue Cross label from the Nitedals factory in Norway. In October that year the factory celebrated its fiftieth anniversary and to mark the occasion printed on its gross size Blue Cross labels '50 Years Anniversary Oct 1955'. There was no such commemorative slogan on the box labels so this was a case where the gross label was a must for every collector — and very difficult to locate, too.

Having decided on how and what to collect the next important matter is identification. A slight overall knowledge of the feel or look of a number of European languages can be a great help here and will enable one to distinguish between, for instance, Polish and Hungarian labels. On the other hand, labels with wording in French could come not only from France but Belgium or even Luxembourg, and German words on a label could denote West or East Germany, Austria, the German-speaking part of Switzerland or, on earlier labels, the Austro-Hungarian Empire. So relying on language alone to identify country of origin is not an infallible method. But there are other ways and perhaps one of the most reliable is to memorise the word for 'matches' in several different languages. Cyrillic and oriental scripts present their own special problems and at first sight it is easy to confuse Georgian (from Russia) with Burmese or Thai. In such cases type and quality of paper, printing, illustration and general lay-out will often assist the collector in determining country of origin, although it must be admitted that such skill is acquired with experience and for the beginner there can be difficulties.

Labels from certain countries always carry distinguishing letters, numbers or symbols. For instance, for many years labels from West Germany have had numbers printed on them, usually in the top left-hand corner. These are the tax control numbers allocated to every factory. It must be remembered, however, that prior to World War II Germany was a united country and so on pre-1939 labels a number could denote a factory situated in either of the two present divisions of West or East. At least 269 different factory numbers have appeared on German labels over the years and one number at least has been used by eight different factories at different times. The numbers range from one to 3,221 although there are many gaps in between and there are the additional M2 and D2.

The reason for the allocation of numbers is puzzling but there is a simple explanation. In the late 1920s and early 1930s Ivar Kreuger, the so-called 'Swedish Match King', controlled much of the match production in Europe, including that in Germany. In the late 1920s, to combat strong competition from the eastern European countries which threatened the German match industry, the Weimar Reoublic negotiated a large loan from Kreuger and in 1930 formed a company — Deutsche Zundwaren-Monopolgesellschaft — to handle all the trading in matches. This was a subdivision of the Finance Ministry in Germany, which still handles the sale, export and import of all matches. Numbers were allocated to all factories at the time of the formation of the company to facilitate organisation and security.

The thinking behind the numbering was strange. For example, between one to 30, numbers 6, 27 and 29 are missing; between 30 and 59 there was no 48 and from 59 the numbers jump to 64 and so on. A further complication is that various authorities supply different sets of numbers for different factories. The German Embassy in London appears to cling to a pre-1939 list for distribution to enquirers, whereas the Trade Ministry in West Germany omits quite a few numbers which are known to exist on labels in collections, and East Germany does not keep any check list at all. It is now almost impossible to identify any one *factory* from a number on a label but still the numbers denote that the labels come from Germany. Labels printed in East Germany since 1945 and destined for the export market usually carry the letter 'R' which denotes the Reisa factory.

Russian labels for home consumption come in great quantity and variety and can often be extremely puzzling. It is helpful to remember that the letters CCCP stand for USSR and the cryptic '50 WT' or '45 WT' or 'WTYK' which often appear on Russian labels, especially on older ones, denote the number of sticks in the box — 50, 45 etc. Cyrillic script on Russian labels can be varied, such as on boxes of matches sold in the region of Georgia, where the script is noticeably different.

Labels are not always what they seem — for example, the French Allumettes de Sureté labels which characterised French matches from 1935 up until a few years ago. They all looked the same and the novice collector could easily be tempted to mount them all under 'France'. But the French match monopoly SEITA (Service d'Exploitation et Industrie des Tabacs et Allumettes which translates as Service for the Development of the Tobacco and Match Industry) placed contracts with a number of countries for the supply of matches and those countries put their identifying letters at the bottom corners of the labels. Again it seems simple but it is not. For instance, 'A' on such a label does not denote, say, Austria, as might be expected—it denotes a Russian origin because it stands for 'Amtorg', the Russian trading company. Austria was denoted by 'Ö' (Österreich) but some of its labels also carried the initials 'SV'—Solo (works) Vienna. Belgium is not always 'B' but also 'UA' (Union Allumettière, the Belgian match company) or 'N' (the Ninove factory). Denmark is not only 'D' but 'G' — standing for H. E. Gosch & Co, the Danish manufacturers. Hungary was 'M' (Magyar) and, just to confuse things even more, 'L' (Lignimpex, the Hungrian trading company). 'E' for Estonia, 'FI' for Finland, 'I' for Italy, and 'P' for Poland are quite straightforward. 'H' means Yugoslavia as it stands for Hempro, the Yugoslavian Trading Corporation, and 'J' denotes the Jönköping factory in Sweden. 'T' represents Czechoslovakia (Tchechslovakie). The same letters printed on other labels marked merely 'Made in Europe' have the same meanings.

(*opposite*)
Part of a traveller's sample sheet of a set of Japanese labels depicting the fifty-five stations of the Tokaido Road

H.H. THE RAJA
—OF DHAR—

H.H. THE THAKIR
—OF LIMRI—

H.H. THE MAHARAJA
—OF JODHPUR—

H.H. THE MAHARAJA
OF BALRAMPUR

H.H. THE MAHARAJA
—OF JDAR—

H.H. THE MAHARAJA
OF KUCH BEHAR

KALI

THE ESAVI INDIA MATCH
FACTORY CALCUTTA

Solo

MADE IN AUSTRIA

WIMCO
SAFETY MATCHES

Old Austrian and Czech labels also carried identifying letters denoting the factory from which they came and among these is 'UA' which stands for the old Austrian factory of Union Augsberg. Swiss labels (which may be printed in French or German) can be recognised by the little symbols in the corners—one a crossbow and the other a curious little device of circles ranged up a stick.

This business of numbers and letters on labels from European countries is often the bane of a collector's life and can confuse the less experienced. As mentioned above, old Austrian and Czech labels carried identifying letters. Up to the year 1916 labels on all match brands manufactured for consumption within the Austro-Hungarian Empire had by law to have the name of the manufacturer printed on them. By 1916 practically all the match factories had been absorbed into two large concerns—Solo and Helios — and in that year duty was introduced to be paid on all matches manufactured in Austria-Hungary. Every factory was bound to put its identifying mark on its labels, thus code letters and numbers such AR, LI, SU, BB, VDP etc, followed by a number, were printed. This combination indicated the factory of origin plus the contents of the box. Up to 1954 these codes appeared on all Czech labels but since that date Czechoslovakian labels have dropped the original code letters and numbers and instead have carried the name of the factory and its location, for instance Solo Sucice, Solo Lipnik, Iskra Ružomberok etc. The Banska Bystrica factory for some reason is not fully included in this otherwise firm rule and it sometimes carried the code Iskra BB. The code letters and numbers came in a variety of permutations and one leading Czechoslovakian collector has informed me that at least forty-five combinations of letters and at least thirteen combinations of numbers have been recorded on labels from

Czechoslovakian and Austrian match factories. The whole spectrum of labels and factories of the former Austro-Hungarian Empire is complicated and to write about it in detail would fill a chapter on its own.

Differentiating between Chinese and Japanese labels is a problem to even the advanced collector, unless one has a knowledge of the respective languages and scripts. Type of printing, paper and general design are factors which can help to determine country of origin but even those are not infallible. Cyrillic script presents some of the same problems, appearing as it does on Russian, Bulgarian and some Yugoslavian labels for the respective home markets. Dutch and Flemish are often confused — one denotes labels from Holland, the other from Belgium, but some words are so similar that a knowledge of both languages is necessary if one is to be sure of classifying correctly.

Name and addresses on labels are not always true guides to country of origin either. One needs to be very careful. For instance, many early Italian labels carry the names and addresses of firms in other countries. In the late nineteenth century there was a very large export trade in matches from Italy and a number of Italian firms exported on behalf of foreign firms. Best known of these was Luigi de Medici, which exported for Roche et Cie of Marseilles and Paris. The pictures were beautifully printed and coloured but were often regarded as decidedly risqué, depicting classical nudes, scantily attired *demi-mondes* and even portraits of famous courtesans of the period. The captions were likewise frowned upon by the more puritanical section of the community but what was then considered to be highly suggestive would today raise no eyebrows at all. Other well known Italian firms included Gand, which exported for Zirold, Brieger and Co, a German company, and whose designs were said to be the most daring.

Identifying marks which are foolproof are the excise number symbols printed on Australian labels. These appear as fractions in a circle, in the past nearly always printed in the top right-hand corner of the label but nowadays wherever they will fit in unobtrusively with the design. The top half of the fraction represents the number allocated to the factory, the lower half relates to the state in which the factory is situated. Of these $1/3$ denotes Bryant & May; $1/4$ is the Federal

Match Co. 3/3 was the old Duncan's factory and now Premier Match Works; 15/1 is W. A. Match Co (West Australian Match Co); 2/4 is Matches (Australia) Ltd; 10/1 is the Australian Match Co Pty Ltd and 3/4 is Safeway Matches Co. These firms are all of fairly recent origin. Even without the excise numbers Australian labels should provide no problems because by law they must always have 'Made in Australia' printed on them.

Labels from Israel should present no great difficulties because Hebrew script is more or less easily recognisable. But to aid identification Israeli factory trade marks include a device like an upturned mushroom, another like a child's drawing of a little house and another which can best be described as an open heart shape enclosing another device which defies description.

Every collector must learn to beware of the fake and it surprises some people to know that there are counterfeit matchbox labels just as there are counterfeit medals, coins, stamps and so on. In label collecting these undesirable items are sometimes referred to more politely as 'reprints' but they remain labels circulating under false colours and are never handled by collectors if they can help it. True reprints are something quite different and perfectly legitimate. The word 'reprint' causes some confusion because obviously some popular brands are reprinted time and time again by the manufacturers as stocks become exhausted. That is why it is far better to use the word 'fake' when referring to dubious labels. It has happened on several occasions in the past that long after a match brand has become obsolete its labels suddenly appear again on the market, usually in mint condition. Excuses are sometimes put forward that a batch of old labels has been discovered in a manufacturer's stock-room or a deceased partner's desk, or some other plausible story, but the truth is that the labels have been printed again, not for the purpose of being stuck on matchboxes for retail sale, but to be circulated among collectors and possibly make quite a sizeable sum of money for some unscrupulous person. It may well be that the original printing blocks have fallen into the wrong hands but it is not unknown for tricksters to have entirely new blocks made.

For the experienced collector fakes are fairly easy to identify, for the novice collector they may be a little more difficult. Points to watch out for are paper which has not faded with time and printing which looks fresh. With modern techniques enabling paper to be 'aged' the spotting of a fake has become slightly harder but there is something unmistakable about mellowed printing and, if seen together, the genuine label and the false one exhibit obvious differences. The famous Swedish Nurseryland sets have been greatly abused in this way, as has the well known American Trotting Horse label and a number of early British labels of the type much sought after by collectors today. Nowadays reputable dealers will always sell reprints as such and some people like to have an example as a curiosity in their collection. One European collector even has a special, separate collection of fake labels, quite an eye-opener for those who have not seen many of these products.

Another thing which it is wise to avoid and with which serious collectors will have no dealings is the collectors' label. This is the same as the collectors' postage stamp — a worthless piece of paper. Such labels are printed (often in sets) solely for the purpose of being sold to collectors at usually exorbitant prices and are never intended to be stuck on matchboxes. None of the large match firms or the reputable smaller ones indulges in this practice; such rubbish is usually produced by individuals for personal gain and it is remarkable how it seems to infiltrate dealers' stocks, exchange packets and private exchanges between collectors, the latter probably being entirely unaware of the nature of the labels, having received them in good faith. In the 1960s and '70s a number of these sets of so-called labels emanated from Belgium, one notorious example being twelve calendar-tab leaves printed in the size of matchbox labels. Long sets from Pakistan and the Dutch East Indies, printed on very thin, poor quality paper, circulated for a number of years and there were even some such items from Poland. Happily the practice has not been so widespread in recent years, possibly because collectors have become more knowledgeable.

These worthless labels are not to be confused with modern 'back' labels which some collectors refuse to handle. The latter are simply advertising stickers, often stuck to the reverse side of a

(opposite) Modern match booklets from Holland, Japan, Canada and Spain

Model Village Babbacombe

CORNISH MATCH COMPANY ST IVES CORNWALL   MADE BY ROSEMATCH JAPAN   CONTESNTS 20

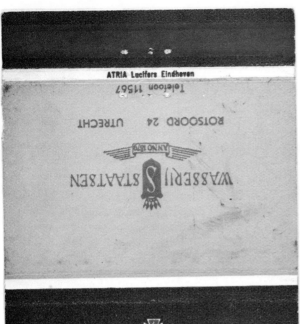

ATRIA Lucifers Eindhoven
Telefoon 11567

ROTSOORD 24   UTRECHT

WASSERIJ STAATSEN   ANNO 1879

CIERRE ANTES DE ENCENDER
GRAL. FOSFORERA, S.A.-AVDA. DEL GENERALISIMO, 51 -MADRID

40 14 62   PALMA DE MALLORCA
(allado Palacio Marivent)
Avda. Joan Miro, 243

CANTON

RESTAURANTE CHINO   CHINESE RESTAURANT

Gracias por su visita

Ph: 525-4731
L8N 1G8
Hamilton, Ontario.
100 Main St., East.
Development-Department.
Regional Planning and

DEVELOPMENT IS OUR THEME

THE REGIONAL MUNICIPALITY OF
HAMILTON WENTWORTH

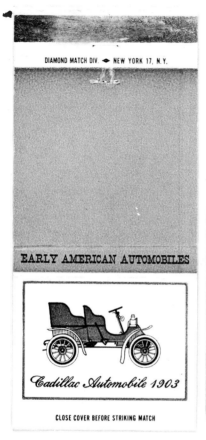

Over the years match booklets (or matchcovers as they are called in America) have come in many different sizes. Sets, such as the 'Early American Automobiles' are very popular

normal matchbox. They are usually printed in black and white and give the name of a café, restaurant, tobacconist's shop etc. They are perfectly legitimate advertising material, printed for the proprietor of the establishment and usually stuck by him on the boxes of ordinary matches before he retails them. Some collectors like to keep them together with the box label, just as a matter of interest; from a true label collecting angle they have no value whatsoever. They should *not* be sent out to other collectors as genuine labels for exchange.

Perhaps the question that one is asked most frequently is about the value of matchbox labels. Someone turns out a collection which they made as a child and thinks it may now be worth a small fortune. Unfortunately, the chances are that it is not. Someone else discovers an old box that grandpa has hoarded and visualises it being sold in auction for several hundred pounds. Again, this can only be a pipe dream.

The question of value is a vexed one. There is no official standard catalogue of matchbox labels as there is with stamps. Dealers often prepare and circulate their own catalogues quoting prices which they would *like* to get; unless they happen to come across a particularly gullible collector or one with little knowledge it is most unlikely that their wildest estimate will be met when it comes to the purchase of an item in question.

The British Matchbox Label and Booklet Society holds regular auctions among its members and perhaps these are the truest guide to the value of certain labels, although in recent years there has been a diminution in the wild bidding which has often in the past pushed items far above their real value. The economic recession has taken its toll in the label world as in everything else.

In Britain the highest prices are probably paid for early British labels and boxes. The continental collectors may push the prices up for early continental labels and boxes which do not find so much favour with British collectors. Putting a price on any particular item is almost an impossibility and extremely misleading. In many cases a label which may be of great value to one person who needs it to complete a set, or because it has specialist interest, may be rated much lower in value by other collectors who do not covet it to the same extent. Inevitably, in auctions people tend to get carried away. For instance in the viewing prior to auction Mr A. may examine a certain label and put his ceiling price for it at £2 but when the auction starts Mr. B., who wants that particular label to complete a set, plunges in with a much higher bid than £2, feeling sure he will then get it. Mr A. immediately thinks that it must be far more desirable than it actually is and so forgets all about his £2 ceiling and bids on. The price rises and the label in question finally reaches a figure for which the buyer is most unlikely to be able to ever sell it again. I have seen many collectors burn their fingers in this way over the years.

As a very rough estimate, early British labels from, say, 1840 to 1890 could be worth up to £20 each, depending on the size and output of the factory which originally issued them and their condition. It is known that higher prices have been paid in some individual cases but if one is of a canny disposition one is forced to think of the old saying 'A fool and his money are soon parted'. In 1981 a continental collector showed me an early French label for which he was asking £50; I rather dumbfounded him by showing him an empty box from the same series, in good condition and infinitely more desirable than a flat label, for which I had paid 50p only eighteen months previously.

So one can only say that prices are fluid and a matter for personal negotiation in cases where a lot of money is being asked. Very old collections (formed prior to 1890) may make a sizeable sum if sold intact. Collections formed in the 1930s and 1940s onwards and consisting mainly of labels current during those periods do not have their value counted in hundreds, let along thousands; depending on the size of the collection of course, they can seldom be recommended as being worth more than a moderate two-figure sum, though some dealers or auctioneering firms will have one believe otherwise.

The occasional rare commemorative label of later period may, of course, create considerable interest if it was a limited issue, as for example a

Bookmatches from Italy

VALQUIRIA

Figura da mitologia escandi-
nava que personificava as vir-
tudes dos heróis.
Mensageira de Odin, tinha por
missão escolher os mais bravos
guerreiros, mortos em com-
bate, e conduzi-los, nos seus
cavalos alados, ao Valhala.

Figuras Equestres — N.º 1

Bookmatches from Portugal

matchbox or matchbox label printed specially for a royal occasion, when perhaps only enough were produced to supply the guests at a banquet. If it can be proved that such a label is a genuine matchbox label and served the purpose for which it was created then its value and the ultimate price paid for it can soar, although not to such dizzy heights as sometimes the press will have us believe.

As with stamps, condition is all important. A clean label in good condition is worth far more than a tattered and torn one. A very old label in poor condition may be worth far less than a much later one in good condition.

There is also the vexed question of comparative values of label or box. Opinions differ on this but my view is that an intact empty matchbox dating from 1830 to 1900 is worth far more than merely the label soaked from the box. There can be no question that an early box with its full complement of matches is more valuable than just the label. It must also be remembered that a complete box of very early matches is often regarded nowadays as an antique in its own right, quite apart from its value to matchbox label collectors. I had an instance of this a few years ago when a titled gentleman presented three boxes of early 'candle matches' to his local church bazaar: a valuable gift which was unfortunately not appreciated by the bazaar organisers at the time and which was in danger of being sold among the rubbish for a very small sum. Fortunately they were rescued in the nick of time by someone who remembered that I collected matchbox labels and I had the opportunity of purchasing them at a sum which was possibly near what the donor had hoped they would realise for church funds. The donor is now dead and his stately home is administered by the National Trust; two boxes of candle matches, identical to the ones which he donated to the bazaar and which are now in my own collection, are on view in the house, shown off behind glass as antiques.

Any hobby is more fun if it is not conducted as a solo undertaking. Contact with other people who have the same interest and the fun of exchanging unwanted items for ones which are new to the collection maintain the momentum and make the hobby doubly exciting. So it is with matchbox labels, and any collector of these trifles who intends to stick with the hobby for some time should certainly consider joining a society.

(*opposite*) American Kitchen Matches will strike any-where, and carry a warning on the box that they should be handled with care and not dropped. This 1982 skillet is one of a set featuring Stoves of Yesteryear

The annual exhibition, held in London in 1948, of the British Matchbox Label & Booklet Society

The author at home with a small part of her extensive collection

The parent body in Great Britain, with tentacles spreading throughout the world, is the British Matchbox Label and Booklet Society, now nearing its fortieth year of existence and growing in stature all the time. Started by a handful of enthusiasts, the BML & BS now has about 2,000 members on its books and over the years many hundreds more have passed through its ranks. It caters for collectors of all age groups and of all degrees of experience, and has an official 'Uncle' to marshal junior members and assist them with their collections. Regular meetings, exhibitions and auctions are held in London and the Society runs a postal bookshop for the sale of the many privately printed items produced by individual members on specialised subjects. It also publishes, six times a year, a thirty-two page magazine which is acknowledged as the leader in its field and which contains a wealth of information in the form of articles, news items, illustrations etc of great interest to both advanced and beginner collectors. Membership fees for this valuable service are reasonable: at the time of writing, £3 per year for adult members, £2 for junior members (up to sixteen years of age) and old age pensioners and £4 for family membership. To obtain full details write to the Membership Secretary, Mr S. Thompson, 3 Langton Close, West Earlham, Norwich, England.

In addition to the BML & BS there are a number of local clubs, many of them affiliated to the parent body, covering such areas as the Medway towns of Kent; East Anglia; the Midlands; the South East of England and so on. These groups meet regularly at local venues and some produce their own news sheets with general label news as well as club information. Overseas there are clubs in a number of European countries as well as in Australia and New Zealand. In the USA there are many clubs which cater for the collectors of bookmatches only, but this is a separate branch of the hobby, as is the collecting of what is known as 'hardware'. This includes match holders of all types, shapes and sizes, from slides into which a box of matches is inserted for protection, to elaborate metal or porcelain contraptions which are ornamental as well as useful, or to the tiny pocket vesta boxes which at one time adorned the watch chain of every self-respecting gentleman.

9

DEVIATIONS FROM THE MAIN THEME

BOOKMATCHES

Brief mention has been made in the previous chapter that the collecting of bookmatches is often regarded as a separate branch of the hobby, and many label collectors do not collect booklets and vice versa. On the other hand the collecting of 'sidelines' is now a significant part of the matchbox scene and no collector's guide could be complete without including some information about the fast growing 'sub-sections' which are now attracting the attention of more and more people who were formerly strictly interested in labels.

When I was working on research for this book I was given invaluable help by the President Emeritus of the University of Cincinnati, Mr Walter C. Langsam, and to him must be credited most of the information concerning bookmatch production.

It is believed that bookmatches were invented in America by Joshua Pusey, a Philadelphia patents attorney, in 1892. He naturally patented the idea but in recent years other, admittedly somewhat flimsy, claims have been put forward concerning the inventor. Be that as it may, Pusey has always been acknowledged as the inventor and until tangible proof can be brought forward to show otherwise he will continue to hold that honour. He called his invention Flexible Matches but the end product was unreliable, some said it was downright dangerous and it did not meet with instant popularity. Pusey held the patent for two years before deciding it was not going to make him his fortune, whereupon he sold it to the Diamond Match Company of America for $4,000, a quite considerable sum of money in those days.

Immediately one of Diamond Match Company's backroom boys, William Armstrong Fairburn, a mechanical and chemical engineer, got to work on the matches and soon made them safe and completely usable. At the end of the nineteenth century the Diamond Match Company, which had been experimenting with a 'ticket tape' match which looked like a roll of caps for a toy pistol, made a great effort to further improve on Fairburn's work and to introduce a more developed product to the public. The striking surface was put on the outside of the book instead of inside the flap, there were twenty matches per book and — the greatest breakthrough of all as it later turned out to be — the outside was used for advertising. It was a match manufacturer's salesman, Henry C. Traute (later to become manager of the bookmatch department of the Diamond Match Company) who is believed to have first suggested the using of bookmatch covers for advertising purposes, although legend has it that the idea was passed to him by someone else.

The first such advertising appeared in a rather unlikely field, that of a high-sounding organisation, The Mendelson Opera Company. The company was a travelling group which staged light musical shows in a revue pattern. When they were booked to give a show in New York someone, maybe the person who gave the idea to Henry Traute, conceived the notion that bookmatch covers could be used to carry advertising for the forthcoming event. It was of the greatest significance, although no one realised it at the time.

So there appeared in very limited quantity a crudely printed matchcover, the copy printed in an illiterate hand and with some spelling mistakes

(opposite) a 1980s set of skillets sold to benefit charity

Limited edition of 5,000 sets.

Nicholas Breakspear (Pope Adrian IV) (died 1159)
The only English Pope. Born at Abbots Langley and educated abroad, his father became a monk in the St. Alban's abbey. Nicholas became Abbot of St. Rufus, near Valence, and was made Cardinal of Albano in 1146, being immediately sent on an embassy to Scandinavia. He was elected Pope in 1154 on the death of Anastasius, and remained in office until his death in 1159. He was noted for his skill and decisiveness and it was he who granted Ireland to Henry-II.

HERTFORDSHIRE ASSOCIATION for the DISABLED

Limited edition of 5,000 sets.

St. Alban
England's first Christian martyr. Reputed to have been born at Verulamium in the latter part of the 3rd century AD, and to have been a soldier in Diocletian's army, he was converted to Christianity by a priest after his return home. On refusing to perform a ceremonial act of worship of Roman deities, he was tortured, then executed on the site of the present Cathedral in c. 303 AD. June 22nd is St. Alban's day.

HERTFORDSHIRE ASSOCIATION for the DISABLED

Limited edition of 5,000 sets.

George Bernard Shaw (1856-1950)
Author and playwright. Born in Dublin, he came to England in 1876 after which he began writing novels, and became music critic for the "Star" in 1888. His first play was performed in 1892 and he wrote a further 35, most of them major works, as well as many other articles and books. He married in 1898, and came to live at Ayot St. Lawrence in 1906 and died here in 1950. "Shaw's Corner" is now the property of the National Trust.

HERTFORDSHIRE ASSOCIATION for the DISABLED

Limited edition of 5,000 sets.

Richard Rumbold (1622-1685)
Extreme republican and chief conspirator in the Rye House plot of 1683. He married a malster's widow and carried on this trade at Rye House. He had been one of the guards at the scaffold of Charles I. Charles II and his brother James were to be assassinated as they passed near Rye House on their way from Newmarket to London, but the plot was frustrated as they set out some days earlier than expected. Rumbold was tried and executed in 1685. Rye House gateway, built in the 15th century, still stands.

HERTFORDSHIRE ASSOCIATION for the DISABLED

Limited edition of 5,000 sets.

Lady Ferrers (1635-1660)
The "Wicked Lady" of Markyate. Traditionally a female highwayman, Katherine Ferrers was married when aged 12 to Sir Thomas Fanshawe of Ware, aged 16, and lived at Markyate Cell. In male attire and riding a black horse with white fore-feet, she robbed travellers on the highway, but was eventually fatally wounded and found dead near a "secret" staircase in the house; she was buried in Ware church. This legend was the subject of a film "The Wicked Lady" in 1945.

HERTFORDSHIRE ASSOCIATION for the DISABLED

but embellished with two pictures — one a portrait of what it called 'America's Youngest Operatic comedian Thomas Lowden' and the other a full-length picture of a person who was supposed to be the show's leading lady but who looked more like a man. The wording on this historic matchcover was 'Wait — We are Coming — Powerful caste Pretty Girls Handsome wardrobe A cyclone of Fun Loof (sic) For The Date Get Seats Early'. On the other panel were the pictures plus 'America's Youngest Operatic comedian Thomas Lowden and the Mendelson Opera Co. Look for the date'. With as much advertising as possible crammed into the limited space, capital letters scattered indiscriminately and the eccentric spelling it was hardly a world-shattering object. But it is believed that several hundred copies of this extraordinary bookmatch cover were produced and today only one is known to exist. It is owned by the Diamond Match Company, which has it insured for an astronomical sum.

However, this crude forerunner of today's slick bookmatches evidently had an effect. The first large order obtained for advertising bookmatch covers was from the Pabst Brewing Company of Milwaukee which wanted 10,000,000 booklets. It was such a promising start that the Diamond factory at Barberton, Ohio, was expanded and adapted for greater production.

Suddenly it was realised that there was a snag. People did not know how to use the new matches in the proper way and the matches were constantly being returned to the manufacturer as not being effective or reliable. But the enterprising Mr Traute rose to the occasion again. He secured an order from the American Tobacco Company for 30,000,000 booklets and to teach people how to use them he had printed on each matchcover the now standard wording 'Close cover before striking match'. This was also the start of the American custom of giving books of matches free to customers, something which has now spread throughout much of the world. It came about because the Metropolitan Tobacco Company of New York sold all the rejected and returned books on behalf of Diamond Match and thus proved that matches which bore an advertisement for one concern could be sold at a low price to another firm for distribution to its customers. Today it is estimated that over three hundred *billion* matches are given away every year in the USA in the form of matchbooks.

Bookmatches are safety matches which will strike only on the specially prepared abrasive surface, unlike some other splint matches which will strike on any rough surface. In the USA and Britain bookmatches are made from paperboard but in some other countries (notably Italy) the matches are made of wood. The manufacture of bookmatches is now fully mechanised: and a machine slices huge rolls of pre-heated cardboard into 'combs' of, usually, sixty or a hundred matches and separates alternate matches so that the heads will not touch in the head-forming process; then the same machine conveys them through the match-head dips.

The combs are then fed into a booking machine. The covers have already had designs printed on them and first the friction material strips are affixed. The covers are then cut into individual books, and match combs are assembled and staples. The books are then packed into various size containers called 'caddies'. For regular or standard size matchbooks a caddy holds fifty books of matches, and fifty caddies are packed into one case for delivery to the customer.

A number of companies in the USA produce bookmatches and each employs a small army of artists to prepare designs to customers' requirements and for the company's own sets and singles. The manufacturers can also provide what are known as standard cuts (ie covers already cut into fancy shapes), so an unusually shaped cover can be printed with specially ordered designs and this, of course, helps to keep down the cost to the customer.

Every year the number of trade names for different sizes or types of matchbooks increases; for example in America there are Jewelite, Matchoramas, Florentines, Cameos etc. and in Britain Sovereigns, Majors etc. The trade name often refers to the finish of the cover, such as flock, laminated, photographic etc, or to the size, ie Majors, Sovereigns, Giant Features and so on.

For collectors the category of matchcovers is all important. No one is very keen on what are usually known as general or national covers, such as those advertising cigarettes and chewing gum, or the stock 'Thank You — Call Again' cover and so on which are available everywhere. Matchcovers produced for use in naval ships or shore establishments, for army or air force camps

Just a few of the many matchboxes issued by public houses

or commemorating special events or occasions are much sought after. In latter years many collectors have set aside a section in their albums for prestige covers such as those produced for distribution to Concorde passengers or for those sailing first class in *QE 2*. The sheer number of matchbooks is so tremendous that very few people collect every one which comes their way, regardless of its subject. The majority of collectors specialise in various well defined groups — hotels, motels, banks, ships, army camps, transportation, country seats, commemoratives, artistic (non-advertising), clubs, colleges, cities and towns, historical places, 'girlies' (scantily dressed models in seductive poses), television and radio stations, restaurants, 'fraternals' (Masonic Lodges etc), political propaganda and so on. The choice is so wide that there is always something to suit everyone and many collectors specialise in more than one group.

In America a cardinal rule applies to the collecting of matchcovers — they must be unused and in absolutely mint condition. This rule does not apply so rigidly in other countries but no American collector will exchange anything for used covers. In Britain a used matchcover, as with a matchbox label, is a guarantee of authenticity and genuine use of the product.

Before being put into a collection matchcovers have the staples removed: this operation is known in the USA as 'shucking', in Britain as 'opening out'. They are then pressed flat and mounted in albums by means of photo-corners or some other type of fixative which will not mark or damage the cover. Some collectors keep covers in card files or in other storage systems because the printing on the inside of the cover is often as important to them as the printing on the outside. However, this a choice for the individual and depends on how much storage space is available.

Another point for a collector to remember is that a matchcover is immediately rendered valueless if the abrasive section is cut off. Years ago quite a number of collectors did indulge in this heinous crime with the result that many rare old matchcovers are now no more than waste paper.

In the USA and Canada there are dozens of clubs and societies which cater for matchcover enthusiasts. Several of these clubs, such as the Rathkamp Matchcover Society and the Trans-Canada Matchcover Club are long-standing and highly organised institutions with nationwide coverage. Conventions are held annually, to which members gravitate from far and wide, and these events, which usually extend over several days, include exhibitions, talks, social get-togethers and, most important of all, the exchanging of matchcovers among members.

In Britain the British Match Label & Booklet Society caters, as its name implies, for matchbook collectors as well as label collectors and devotes one of its exhibitions through the year to bookmatches only. However, the hobby of matchcover collecting is not pursued on anything like such a large scale as in America; in Britain matchcover collectors are in the minority, although interest is growing and most serious British collectors belong to one or more American clubs. With an estimated million books of matches an hour being handed out free to customers in the United States it can easily be seen that starting a collection does not present any difficulties.

The upsurge of the bookmatch is really remarkable when one considers that originally such matches were so dangerous (they flamed so suddenly that fingers were burnt, they dropped globules of fire from the book and the ends continued glowing after the match had been discarded) and that William Fairburn had at one stage been instructed to terminate bookmatch operations at the giant Diamond Match Company factory, as the management believed that such matches were unprofitable and could never be made or sold economically or guaranteed safe. It was only Henry Traute's faith in them that ensured their survival.

Every president of the USA since the elder Taft has had special matchcovers printed to give away as bookmatches and it was in 1900 that the first American political bookmatch appeared. It was handed out by a Pennsylvanian who stood for Congress and whose slogan 'From Plowboy to Successful Businessman' was printed on his personal matchcovers. Nowadays almost every political candidate in the USA has special matchcovers printed when running in an election and doubtless it is a form of publicity which is very effective. There is probably no commercial undertaking in the USA, from the one-man business to the giant corporations, which has not at some time had its own matchcover printed to advertise its business and this idea is becoming popular in many other parts of the world. In

Royal occasions always provide scope for popular matchbox labels, and match manufacturers had a field day at the time of Prince Charles' wedding

London, for instance, one large department store will print matchcovers with your own name, while you wait, and will present them to you already boxed as books of matches ready for distribution to friends. Whereas at one time only very important people would have special matchcovers for special occasions now it seems no town or country wedding can be absolutely up to date unless matchbooks bearing the names of the bride and groom are distributed at the reception. For some reason these personal covers have never been highly popular with collectors, unless the person concerned happens to be a celebrity.

HARDWARE

I always feel that this is a remarkably unattractive name for a very attractive branch of the match hobby.

The title 'hardware' covers a vast range of objects, made in materials varying from gold to tin or wood and even stone, intended to be carried in the pocket or to stand on anything from an occasional table to a bar counter but all serving the same purpose — to hold matches and usually to provide a striking surface for them. The term has recently been widened by some people to include such 'fringe' items as the cylindrical tins in which wax tapers were sold and a few other ancillary objects.

It must be appreciated that today many match holders are classed as antiques in their own right; they therefore command market prices for the materials in which they are fashioned and are not always bought by matchbox collectors. That does not, however, mean that they are outside the financial scope of even the young collector. Unusual and very worthwhile items quite often turn up in junk shops or on market stalls, for sale at ridiculously low prices simply because the vendor does not appreciate what they are. Quite recently I purchased for 50p a charming mid-nineteenth-century holder for wax matches. The good lady in charge of the secondhand shop, anxious to get rid of some of the accumulation of junk in her cluttered premises, assured me it was 'a little stud box dear, nice for keeping oddments on the dressing table'! Another lucky buy at an auction sale of house contents was one of the ashtray-cum-match-striker contrivances which were fixed to the backs of the upper-deck seats of the old trams in a west country city. Enquiries before the sale started revealed that this specimen, lovingly mounted on a polished wood plaque, had been rescued by a former tram driver when the trams were being broken up and had been treasured by him as a sentimental souvenir. It was the transport connection which pushed the price up to £4 but as an unusual piece of match hardware it was well worth it.

Hardware can range from such comparatively modern trifles to valuable early Instantaneous Light Boxes and historic apparatus such as the Electro-Pneumatic Lamp. These and other pre-match contrivances which attract the attention of museums when they come up (very infrequently) for sale, are handled by world famous auctioneering firms and fetch very high prices often beyond the range of the average matchbox collector. A most interesting item which I saw in a French country-house sale some years ago was a tin box which had been covered with a sixteenth-century portolan (harbour-finding chart) on vellum: it was sold for over £15,000, and that was twenty years ago. Its value today would probably

Greetings for a
"Matchless" Xmas & a
"Striking" New Year.

"SHIP"SAFETY MATCH
AVERAGE 50 CONTENTS
MADE IN SWEDEN
SWEDISH MATCH CO.

AS YOU GO CONDESCENDING,
IN SEARCH EVER BENDING,
TO PICK UP A LABEL THAT'S NEW,
GOOD LUCK NEVER ENDING,
IS THE WISH I AM SENDING
TO THE B.M.L.S. AND TO YOU.

H. ULUNDI-BATHE.
II. OXFORD STREET,
SWINDON,
WILTS.

XMAS 1945.

Typical examples of label ephemera: *(left)* A Christmas card sent by one well-known collector to another and *(opposite)* A 1948 Exhibition programme

be doubled. The value to the buyer was in the portolan, he was not particularly interested in the little bottle for sulphuric acid and the crude little match splints which the box contained, whereas to me that was where its importance lay.

As with all branches of matchbox collecting there is plenty of scope for specialisation in hardware. Some people collect only slides — the protective covers in to which a box of matches is inserted — or match holders in wood, in metal or in pottery and china. Others may go for the even more specialised group of slides which were made by servicemen and prisoners of war in France during World War I, using metal from shell cases and ornamenting the front with perhaps a military badge or button or with a crude design hammered out with a nail. Some collectors seek only holders which advertised such things as whiskey and beer or they may be attracted to pocket and watch chain vesta cases. The latter came in a wide variety of shapes from representations of animals' heads to figures of Punch.

THE BRITISH
MATCHBOX LABEL
AND
BOOKLET SOCIETY

THIRD

ANNUAL EXHIBITION

AT

THE BONNINGTON HOTEL

LONDON

SATURDAY, 10th APRIL, 1948

AND

SUNDAY, 11th APRIL, 1948

PROGRAMME   PRICE 3d.

(KEEP THIS PROGRAMME—IT MAY HAVE THE LUCKY NUMBER)

Tre Stjärnor eller Three Stars den kanske mest känd etiketten av dem alla som tillverkades första gången omkring år 1885 av C. F. Wennberg, ägare av Jönköpings Westra Tändsticksfabrik vid denna tid. Denna etikett är såld över hela världen sedan dess och är fortfarande ett stort varumärke på hemma- och exportmarknaden. Denna typ är ifrån 1917 då S. T. A. B. koncernen övertog marknaden och under åren lär det ha tillverkats cirka 900 varianter av detta varumärke.

2289

Hardware is a wide open field in which the individual collector can turn whichever way he or she feels inclined. One word of warning though — match holders take up a lot more space in the home than matchbox labels!

EPHEMERA

This is the newest branch of the match hobby to claim the attention of collectors. Although for years many collectors have kept, as ancillary to their label collections, news cuttings, leaflets etc dealing with matches and matchbox labels, it is only in recent years that a serious search for ephemera has begun and the whole subject has been opened up. One example of the growing popularity of match ephemera is that people are now willing to *buy* such items, and often for quite high prices, whereas in the past they usually gathered only what was thrown away or was perhaps given to them as likely to be of interest to a match label collector. Now everything has its price and I was recently offered £2 for a Morelands cardboard carton in which I store some flower-arranging material.

In the matchbox world the word 'ephemera' applies to just about anything written or printed on paper or cardboard—except matchbox labels themselves—so anyone who goes in for this offshoot of the hobby has a vast area awaiting exploration and collection. Cartons in which wholesale consignments of matches are delivered are bulky to keep (unless one uses them for the purpose of storing other items): much less space-consuming are such things as billheads, advertisement leaflets and letters. Some years ago a series of comic postcards was issued, featuring drawings which had a small piece of sandpaper stuck to some part of them and usually a mildly vulgar caption; for instance, one showed a man leading a donkey, the animal having a strip of sandpaper stuck across its middle and the caption 'Strike my . . . .'. These postcards which originally sold for about 2d (just under 1p) are now much sought

after by collectors and change hands at several pounds each.

At the other end of the scale match firms' records are highly prized and can range from an invoice for a delivery of matches to company documents. For example, I greatly value a complete confidential file concerning a set of labels printed specially for a firm which, after initial success, ended up as a project which went sadly wrong. It is fascinating when going through the thick sheaf of papers to see how correspondence was extremely cordial at the beginning, becoming even more friendly and appreciative as the special issue got under weigh but towards the end getting shorter and much cooler in tone, finally ending as curt and acrimonious and closing altogether the dealing between the two firms involved. Such a gem of ephemera as this came into my hands only because the head of the firm for which the labels were produced is a personal friend and he generously donated the whole file in the interests of match firm and match label production history. Usually one has to be content with more easily obtainable items which were freely available in their day, such as advertising material and the free bookmarks and postcards with which some of the bigger match firms at one time showered their customers.

MATCH TAX STAMPS

Possibly the least collected items of the match scene are tax stamps. These balance rather uncertainly between philately and matchbox label collecting. Some specialised stamp catalogues include them, but no one has ever catalogued them, as far as is known, in the match label world. They are not easy to come by but provide an interesting study if one is prepared to delve deeply into the subject.

Several countries, notably Italy and South America at the time of writing, raise revenue by a tax on matches. The custom of using match tax stamps started in the USA after the Civil War of 1861–5, and it has been noted that almost all countries in which match tax stamps have been issued introduced them after a war in order to collect the revenue needed to finance the undertaking.

Britain has never had match tax stamps although it came within a whisker of having them in 1871. In that year the Chancellor of the

(*opposite*) Something new to collect. In 1981 the Jönköping match factory in Sweden produced a series of postcards reproducing some of the firm's best known early labels and with a potted history of the brand on the back of each card

Domestic 'war'. The infamous match tax brought forward by Sir Robert Lowe, Chancellor of the Exchequer, in 1871, was never introduced because of the outcry against it. But the match tax stamps were printed in readiness for the introduction of the tax and were never used

Exchequer, Sir Robert Lowe, proposed a tax on matches but the proposal instantly met a storm of protest. Sir Robert earned the title of 'Match Bob' and so vehement was the opposition that the tax was never brought in. Nevertheless, it was a close thing; the revenue stamps were printed and issued to match firms and Bryant & May possesses among its records and museum exhibits an unperforated sheet of twenty-four stamps, value ½d each. The stamps, printed in pale blue-grey, have in the centre a design of a flaming torch within an oval and the inscription 'Ex Luce Lucellum'. This sheet is believed to be unique. Because of the apparently certain introduction of the Match Tax Bill, Bryant & May prepared to put on the market its Exchequer Match. The label was of buff paper, printed with designs in black for three sides of the box; an all-round label in fact. On the front, tucked away down in the corner, was a representation of the earliest type of ½d postage stamp and on the bottom of the box the label carried a crude and very unflattering portrait of Sir Robert Lowe. But these labels were never used; again, Bryant & May has preserved copies among its company documents. Not to be thwarted, however, the firm hastily had a re-think and brought out instead its Bryant & May's Chancellor Matches, again with a representation of the ½d

revenue stamp but on one side of the box the words 'Match-Tax Bill, Introduced 20th April 1871' and on the other side panel 'Withdrawn 25th April 1871'. Incidentally, a big factor in the withdrawal of the proposal was a demonstration against it staged by Bryant & May employees. A tax of ½d a box on matches seems of little consequence these days; over a hundred years ago it would have played havoc with many family budgets. Bryant & May's successful opposition to the tax was so highly applauded by the general public that a commemorative drinking fountain was erected in Bow Road, London, near the Bryant & May factory. The fountain and its erection were paid for by public subscription and it was unveiled by the Lord Mayor of London the year after the withdrawal of the Bill.

In America match tax stamps were used much more extensively than anywhere else and they were continued until 1885–6. A law prohibited the transport of matches by rail and consequently there were a great number of small factories throughout the states, each allowed to have its own stamp: hence the wide and colourful variety. A further addition to the avalanche of collectable material was created by the fact that factories changed hands fairly frequently, necessitating stamps being re-engraved with the name and often the portrait of the new owner. The engraving was usually of a high standard and the stamps themselves very well produced.

There is the keenest interest in these stamps in America, where they are eagerly sought by collectors. They are known there as private die proprietary stamps and the people who collect them are usually philatelists and not matchbox label enthusiasts.

These then are the options open to matchbox label/matchbox/bookmatch collectors, many of whom also go in for the related hardware and ephemera, perhaps just because it happens to come their way, as a fascinating sideline to their main and/or specialised branch of the hobby. Even the non-collector agrees that there seems to be something in it for everybody.

INDEX